A Practical Guide to Detect GenAI

by Dr. Lele Cao

Revision History

March 2025:   First Edition

Preface

The rapid advancement of generative artificial intelligence (AI) technologies has transformed the landscape of digital content creation, leading to remarkably realistic synthetic text, images, videos, audio, and music. While these developments offer tremendous potential for creativity and innovation, they also pose significant threats, including misinformation, identity fraud, and copyright infringement. This practical guide provides a comprehensive overview of current methodologies, techniques, and tools for detecting AI-generated content across various modalities. Structured into three focused chapters, it covers textual, visual, and auditory domains separately, exploring why detection is crucial, how AI-generated content differs from authentic media, and what state-of-the-art techniques are available for effective identification. Readers will learn about vulnerabilities in detection methods and practical strategies to overcome them, accompanied by real-world examples and an overview of publicly available and commercial detection tools. By equipping readers with actionable insights, this synthesis article serves as an essential resource for practitioners, researchers, and stakeholders committed to maintaining the integrity and authenticity of digital information in an AI-driven era.

Contents

1

Detecting AI-Generated Text

Generative AI (GenAI) has significantly advanced in recent years, particularly in generating human-like text through large language models (LLMs). However, the ability of these LLMs to produce indistinguishable text from human writing poses various challenges and risks.

In this chapter, we introduce the critical need for detecting AI-generated text, exploring diverse methods and tools designed for this purpose. By the end of this chapter, you will be equipped with knowledge on how to effectively identify AI-generated content, ensuring the integrity and authenticity of digital information.

In this chapter, we're going to cover the following main topics:

- Why and when do we need to detect LLM-generated text?

- Techniques in AI-Generated text detection: a practitioner's guide.

- Strategies to overcome vulnerabilities in AI-generated text detection.

- A glance of public and commercial tools.

Technical requirements

To effectively engage with the content of this chapter, you will need access to some required technologies and installations:

- Python 3.8 or later.

- Access to OpenAI's GPT-3.5 or later versions.

- Installation of the `transformers` library from HuggingFace.

- Installation of the `torch` library for PyTorch.

Make sure that these prerequisites are set up in your working environment prior to following along with the practical examples we will walk through in this chapter.

Why and when do we need to detect LLM-generated text?

The rapid advancement of LLMs and their ability to generate human-like text have brought significant benefits and posed substantial risks. Recently, many researchers (Chaka, 2024; Crothers, Japkowicz, & Viktor, 2023; Tang, Chuang, & Hu, 2024; Valiaiev, 2024; Wu et al., 2024; Yang et al., 2023) have emphasized the importance of detecting AI-generated content to address these challenges and maintain the integrity of information across different domains. Here, we present a consolidated view of the motivations for detecting AI-generated text.

Key reasons for detecting AI-generated text

Combating misinformation and bias: The proliferation of LLMs has significantly increased the risk of misinformation and fake news, which can mislead the public and cause widespread harm. Detecting AI-generated text helps mitigate these risks and maintain the integrity of information. Additionally, LLMs can generate biased or harmful content, exacerbating social issues such as gender bias and discrimination. Detection tools help identify and mitigate these biases, contributing to a more equitable digital environment.

Upholding academic and scientific integrity: AI-generated texts can easily be used to produce essays, research papers, and other academic content, leading to issues of academic dishonesty and plagiarism. Ensuring that the content submitted by students and researchers is their original work is crucial for maintaining the credibility of educational institutions and the value of academic qualifications. Additionally, AI tools can generate credible-looking research papers, such as (Zhang, Wu, Yang, Zhu, & Liu, 2024), that may contain fabricated findings, undermining trust in scientific publications. Detecting AI-generated content helps maintain the authenticity and reliability of scientific literature.

Preserving trust in digital content: The increasing presence of LLM-generated content on user-accessible platforms can undermine trust in AI systems and digital content.

Effective detection of AI-generated text helps maintain the trustworthiness of published information via online and traditional media.

Safeguarding LLM development: The recursive use of AI-generated text in training data can lead to homogenization and reduced diversity in future models, a phenomenon known as model collapse (Shumailov et al., 2024). Detecting AI-generated text prevents this self-consuming paradigm, ensuring the long-term development and improvement of LLMs.

Promoting educational fairness and critical thinking: AI-generated texts can create an unfair advantage for students who use these tools to complete their assignments or exams, skewing the assessment of their actual understanding and capabilities. Detecting such content ensures a level playing field for all students. Additionally, over-reliance on AI-generated content can negatively impact the learning process by preventing students from developing critical thinking, writing, and research skills. As Ben Feringa, Nobel Prize laureate in Chemistry 2016, emphasized, *"the struggle in writing a good essay is essential to critical thinking"* (Nobel Prize Dialogue: Fact & Fiction - The Future of Democracy, 2024). Detecting and discouraging the use of AI-generated texts encourages deeper engagement with learning material.

Enhancing Cybersecurity and Content Moderation: AI-generated text can be used in phishing attacks and other malicious activities. Detecting such content enhances cybersecurity measures and protects users from fraud and other online threats. Additionally, on online platforms such as social media, AI-generated text can contribute to spam, fake reviews, and bot-generated comments, undermining the quality and reliability of user-generated content. Detection tools help maintain the authenticity of online discourse.

Guarantee legal and ethical compliance: The widespread use of LLM-generated text in creative fields raises significant legal issues regarding Intellectual Property (IP) rights. Detecting AI-generated content is crucial for distinguishing human creativity from machine-generated outputs, which is essential for developing robust frameworks to guarantee legal compliance. Additionally, ensuring that AI systems are developed and used ethically, lawfully, and robustly is crucial. Detecting AI-generated text helps maintain fairness, robustness, and accountability in AI systems.

Address societal impact and public awareness: The influence of advanced language models on various sectors, including journalism, customer service, and academia, necessitates a deeper understanding of their socio-technological ramifications. Effective detection systems are essential to mitigate potential negative impacts on society. Additionally, increasing public awareness and AI literacy (Ng, Leung, Chu, & Qiao, 2021) regarding AI-generated content is crucial for responsible and sustainable usage. The general population needs to be better equipped to deal with the influx of AI-generated text, ensuring individuals can critically evaluate and discern the authenticity of the information they encounter.

Situations where detection may not be necessary?

It is worth pointing out that not all situations require the detection of LLM-generated text, as unnecessary detection can lead to system inefficiencies and inflated development costs (Wu et al., 2024). Here are some scenarios where detection may not be necessary:

- The use of LLMs involves minimal risk, especially when they are employed for routine, repetitive tasks.

- The spread of LLM-generated text is restricted to predictable, limited domains, such as closed information circles with few participants.

- In educational settings where AI tools are leveraged to augment learning and are openly integrated into the curriculum.

- The content generated by LLMs is used for creative or experimental purposes, where AI contribution is acknowledged and valued.

As we consider the importance and limitations of detecting AI-generated text, it is essential to explore the various techniques available for practitioners. In the next section, we will walk through key methods and tools for detecting AI-generated content, examining both their strengths and challenges.

Techniques in AI-Generated text detection: a practitioner's guide

Despite the rapid evolution of AI-generated text detection, we provide a systematic walkthrough of various detector designs and algorithms from a practitioner's perspective. Recently, Tang, Chuang, and Hu (2023) proposed categorizing detection methods into two broad categories: **black-box detection** and **white-box detection**. Black-box detection methods identify AI-generated text without needing access to the internal workings of the language model. They rely on analyzing the text's external features and patterns to find indicators of AI generation. In contrast, white-box detection methods require access to the model's internal parameters and mechanisms. These methods use detailed insights into the model's architecture to detect AI-generated content more accurately. While white-box detection can offer higher precision, it is limited by the need for access to the source model. In this chapter, we focus on the most recently proposed methods and provide a more granular categorization framework based on their underlying design principles.

LLM prompting: fighting fire with fire

Detecting AI-generated text by directly prompting LLMs is a simple and popular method, often employing **black-box** and **zero-shot** detection techniques. Zero-shot detection refers to the ability to identify AI-generated text without having been specifically trained on examples of such text. The methods in this category leverage the LLM's capabilities by prompting it to distinguish between human and AI-generated text, utilizing the model's understanding to detect generated content. Recent research has extensively explored this method, highlighting both its potential and challenges. In principle, they involve crafting prompts that instruct the model to classify the text as either AI-generated or human-written. Therefore, the main effort lies in prompt engineering, which involves many variations as demonstrated by recent works such as (Bhattacharjee & Liu, 2024; Mireshghallah, Mattern, Gao, Shokri, & Berg-Kirkpatrick, 2024; Taguchi, Gu, & Sakurai, 2024; Zhang et al., 2024). By analyzing the model's responses, we can determine the likelihood of the text being AI-generated. This method is particularly appealing because it does not require access to the internal working mechanisms of the model, making it easily and broadly applicable across different models and text types.

Let's walkthrough the approach studied in (Bhattacharjee & Liu, 2024), which demonstrates how to use GPT-3.5 as an AI-generated text detector by prompting the model to classify a given text as either human-written or AI-generated. Following these steps will show you how to set up and execute a detection prompt using LLMs.

1. Import the necessary library and set the OpenAI API key.

```
import openai
openai.api_key = "YOUR_OPENAI_API_KEY"
```

2. Define the text sample to be tested and set the LLM parameters. In this example, we choose GPT-3.5 as our detector LLM and set the maximum number of output tokens to 1024.

```
text_sample = "The quick brown fox jumps over the lazy
dog."
model_engine = "gpt-3.5-turbo"
max_tokens = 1024
```

3. Define the prompt for the LLM detector.

```
prompt = f"Is the following passage generated by an AI or
written by a human: '{text_sample}'"
```

4. Send the prompt to LLM and print the response.

```
completion = openai.ChatCompletion.create(
  model=model_engine,
  messages=[{'role': 'user', 'content': prompt}],
  max_tokens=max_tokens
)
print(completion.choices[0].message.content)
```

Detecting AI-generated text with LLM prompting presents a range of challenges and insights. Here, we discuss the key points derived from recent research, providing a comprehensive overview of this method's potential and limitations.

One significant challenge lies in the *evolving sophistication of LLMs* and the *crucial role of prompt engineering*. As highlighted by Zhang et al. (2024), detectors in this category often struggle with adapting to newer, more advanced models like ChatGPT-4. The effectiveness of detection methods diminishes significantly when encountering text generated by these advanced models or when prompts (for generating the texts to be tested) are intentionally designed to vary writing styles. Zhang et al. (2024) underscore the need for more robust and adaptive detection methods that can keep pace with the rapid advancements in LLM capabilities.

Another major challenge identified by Bhattacharjee and Liu (2024) is the *high rate of false negatives* (false negatives occur when AI-generated text is misclassified as human-written), particularly when dealing with text from newer, larger models. The variability in detection accuracy based on the adopted prompt further complicates the detection process, with simpler prompts often yielding better results. Interestingly, while GPT-3.5 struggles with AI text, it is more reliable in recognizing human-written text, and thus potentially solves the problem of AI-generated text detection, albeit in an indirect way. Conversely, GPT-4 tends to misclassify human-written text from TuringBench dataset (Uchendu, Ma, Le, Zhang, & Lee, 2021), highlighting its *sensitivity to dataset noise and LLM varieties*.

Interestingly, Mireshghallah et al. (2024) explores the *effectiveness of smaller language models* in detecting AI-generated text. The study finds that smaller models, such as OPT-125M (Zhang et al., 2022), outperform larger models in detecting machine-generated text across different LLM generators. This is attributed to the higher curvature and likelihood values that smaller models assign to machine-generated text compared to human-written text. Additionally, partially trained models can sometimes be more effective detectors than fully trained ones. These findings suggest that smaller models offer a more robust and generalizable solution for zero-shot detection, providing an alternative approach to leveraging LLMs.

Taguchi, Gu, and Sakurai (2024) highlights that current zero-shot detectors often analyze texts in isolation, ignoring the prompts that generated these texts, leading to discrepancies in likelihood evaluations. By incorporating those prompts in the detection process, **white-box** *LLM prompting methods* significantly improve the detection accuracy. This finding emphasizes the importance of considering text-generating prompts in detection methodologies and suggests that exploring the effects of different text lengths, parameter sizes, and benign tasks (such as summarization, paraphrasing, and translation) can be beneficial.

In summary, while LLM prompting methods show certain promise due to its broad applicability and ease of use, several challenges remain. These include the need for adaptive and robust detection methods to keep up with evolving LLM capabilities, addressing high rates of false negatives, leveraging smaller models for zero-shot detection, and exploring white-box methodological variations.

Linguistic and statistical methods

Detection methods relying on linguistic and statistical indicators are crucial for identifying AI-generated texts. These techniques compute linguistic properties and statistical regularities to distinguish between human and machine-generated content. These methods can be classified into white-box and black-box approaches, depending on whether they require access to the internal mechanics of the language models (white-box) or treat them as opaque systems (black-box).

White-box statistical methods leverage detailed information about LLM's operations to identify AI-generated text. One high-level intuition is to measure and compare the likelihood of generating some given words. For example, GLTR (Gehrmann, Strobelt, and Rush, 2019) and DetectLLM (Su et al., 2023). More sophisticated white-box techniques include perturbation-based methods, which slightly alter the input text and observe changes in LLM's output probabilities. DetectGPT (Mitchell et al., 2023) and its improved version, Fast-DetectGPT (Bao et al., 2024), exemplify this. Based on the belief that the structure of text can reveal its origins, Tulchinskii et al. (2023) proposed a different detection method using the intrinsic dimensionality of texts. In layman's terms, intrinsic dimensionality refers to the complexity of the text structure when it is represented as points in a high-dimensional space. Another recent innovation, Binoculars (Hans et al., 2024), compares how surprising a piece of text is to two different language models; if the text seems similarly unsurprising to both models, it's likely AI-generated, whereas a greater difference suggests it's human-written.

In contrast, **black-box statistical methods** do not require access to the internal workings of LLMs and calculate external statistical features to identify AI-generated text. One common approach involves continuing a given text using the model and comparing the continuation with the original text. For example, Yang et al. (2024) examine differences in n-gram patterns — sequences of n consecutive words — to detect AI generation. Other methods compute the similarity scores between the original and edited versions of the text, leveraging the observation that human-written texts trigger more extensive edits when revised by AI systems (Mao et al., 2024). Furthermore, some black-box approaches use denoising techniques. These methods introduce noise into a text and then use an AI model to remove it. By comparing the denoised text to the original, they can detect characteristics unique to AI-generated content (Guo and Yu, 2023).

Without even accessing LLMs in either white-box or black-box manner, *linguistic features* can be used to facilitate the detection of AI texts by analyzing specific linguistic properties and statistical regularities within the text. Examples of these features include branching properties in grammatical analysis, function word density (Corston-Oliver, Gamon, and Brockett, 2001), n-gram similarities (Hamed and Wu, 2023), information density (Venkatraman, Uchendu, & Lee, 2024), writing style (Soto et al., 2024), and grammar error corrections (Wu et al., 2024).

Now, let's run through the Binoculars method (Hans et al., 2024) as an example: , which demonstrates how to use two pre-trained language models to calculate perplexity and cross-entropy scores in order to determine whether a text is AI-generated or human-crafted. By following these steps, you will learn how to compute the Binoculars score and interpret the results to classify the text.

1. Import Pytorch and the required libraries from HuggingFace transformers library.

```
import torch
from transformers import AutoModelForCausalLM,
AutoTokenizer
```

2. Load the observer (`tiiuae/falcon-7b`) and performer (`tiiuae/falcon-7b-instruct`) pre-trained language models and the tokenizer.

```
observer_model = AutoModelForCausalLM.from_pretrained(
   "tiiuae/falcon-7b").eval()
performer_model = AutoModelForCausalLM.from_pretrained(
   "tiiuae/falcon-7b-instruct").eval()
tokenizer = AutoTokenizer.from_pretrained(
   "tiiuae/falcon-7b")
```

3. Define and tokenize the text to be tested.

```
input_text = "Dr. Capy Cosmos, a capybara unlike any other,
astounded the scientific community with his groundbreaking
research in astrophysics."
encodings = tokenizer(
   [input_text], return_tensors="pt", padding=True)
```

4. Obtain the output logits from both language models.

```
with torch.no_grad():
   observer_logits = observer_model(**encodings).logits
   performer_logits = performer_model(**encodings).logits
```

5. Compute the perplexity (PPL) for the performer model. Perplexity measures how well a language model expects the next word in a text, with lower values indicating better accuracy.

```
shift_logits = performer_logits[..., :-1, :].contiguous()
shift_labels = encodings['input_ids'][..., 1:].contiguous()
loss_fct = torch.nn.CrossEntropyLoss(reduction='none')
loss = loss_fct(shift_logits.view(-1, shift_logits.size(-
1)), shift_labels.view(-1))
ppl = torch.exp(loss.mean())
```

6. Calculate the cross-entropy (X-PPL) score between the observer and performer models. This step tries to measure how surprising the text is to the observer model compared to the performer model.

```
shift_logits = observer_logits[..., :-1, :].contiguous()
cross_entropy = loss_fct(
  shift_logits.view(-1, shift_logits.size(-1)),
  shift_labels.view(-1)
)
x_ppl = torch.exp(cross_entropy.mean())
```

7. Calculate and print the Binoculars score by dividing PPL by X-PPL.

```
binoculars_score = ppl / x_ppl
print("Binoculars Score:", binoculars_score.item())
```

8. Predict if the text is AI-generated or human-crafted by comparing the Binoculars score to the threshold recommended statistically by (Hans et al., 2024).

```
threshold = 0.9015310749276843
if binoculars_score < threshold:
  print("Most likely AI-generated.")
else:
  print("Most likely human-crafted.")
```

Detection methods relying on linguistic and statistical indicators face several significant challenges that impact their effectiveness and reliability. These challenges stem from the inherent complexities of language, the evolving nature of language models (discussed previously for LLM prompting methods), and the practicalities of deploying these methods in real-world scenarios.

Firstly, the effectiveness of these methods *heavily relies on large datasets* to derive accurate thresholds and patterns. This reliance can make the methods less effective when applied to smaller or less representative datasets. For instance, techniques that compute word frequency (Kalinichenko et al., 2003) or *n*-gram patterns (Gallé et al., 2021) require substantial amounts of data to produce reliable results, otherwise they may fail to accurately distinguish between human and AI composed texts.

Sensitivity to text perturbations poses an obstacle as well – Many statistical methods struggle with texts that have been slightly modified or paraphrased. Techniques that leverage paraphrasing or introducing small grammatical errors, such as (Guo and Yu, 2023), can significantly reduce the accuracy of these detection methods. Adversarial attacks that subtly alter the text to evade detection systems highlight the need for robust detection mechanisms in this category.

A major practical challenge is *scalability and efficiency*. Detecting machine-generated text in real-time or on large-scale platforms, such as social media, requires efficient algorithms that can handle vast amounts of data quickly without significant computational overhead. Methods that rely on sophisticated feature extraction, such as the calculation of Binoculars approach (Hans et al., 2024) demoed earlier, can be computationally expensive and may need refinement before they are suitable for real-time applications.

Bias and fairness are constantly raised as crucial concerns. The statistical/linguistic detection systems can exhibit biases due to statistical outliers, such as incorrectly flagging text from non-native speakers or specific dialects as AI-generated. Ensuring fairness and minimizing false positives is essential to maintain user trust and avoid discrimination. Detection methods must be carefully evaluated and calibrated to prevent unfairly penalizing certain groups of users.

In conclusion, while linguistic and statistical methods for detecting AI-generated texts face some major challenges, ongoing research and innovations continue to improve their robustness, adaptability, and efficiency. By addressing these challenges, these methods can play a crucial role in maintaining the integrity of online platforms, protecting against misinformation, and achieving fair and accurate detection of AI-generated content.

Training-based methods

Training-based methods differ from other detection approaches as they involve training, or sometimes fine-tuning pre-trained language models, to develop detection models using specific datasets. Depending on the nature of training procedure, these methods can be categorized into standard classification, adversarial, and contrastive methods.

Standard classification methods intend to train (often in a supervised fashion) a classifier model that can distinguish between human-written and AI-generated texts. There are largely two subcategories:

- Training classifiers from engineered features.
- Fine-tuning from a pre-trained language model.

The first subcategory involves extracting features from the text, such as word length or frequency (Shah et al., 2023), token perplexity (Li et al., 2023), text provenance (Wang et al., 2023) and lexical richness (Kumarage et al., 2023), and then using these features to train a classifier. The second subcategory builds upon powerful pre-trained language models such as RoBERTa (Liu et al., 2019) and T5 (Raffel et al., 2020), which are fine-tuned on textual datasets annotated with human/machine-generated labels; some well known example methods include OpenAI's text classifier (OpenAI, 2023), GPT-Sentinel (Chen et al., 2023), GPTZero (Tian et al., 2024), Segment-then-Classify (Zeng et al., 2024), and so on.

Adversarial methods refer to techniques that enhance the robustness of detection models by deliberately exposing the training process to challenging, deceptive inputs known as adversarial examples. "**Adversarial**" means applying a competition where one part of the system tries to trick the other. This competition helps the system become better at recognizing these tricky inputs. Within the context of AI-generated text detection, adversarial methods typically involve creating deceptive text samples that mimic human writing but are actually generated by machines. These deceptive samples are used to train and fine-tune the detection models, making them more resilient to challenging detection cases (Yang et al., 2023; He et al., 2023; Shi et al., 2024). Another paradigm, Two-Player Games (Wu et al., 2024), involves training an attack model alongside a detection model. The attack model learns to paraphrase text to deceive the evolving detector model; and the continuous confrontation between them dynamically enhances the detection capability throughout the entire training process. Approaches such as RADAR (Hu, Chen, and Ho 2023) and OUTFOX (Koike, Kaneko, and Okazaki 2023) exemplify this approach.

Contrastive methods focus on learning effective representations, which are essentially numerical vectors derived from a language model (to be fine-tuned) and used as input features for detecting AI-generated texts. These methods typically involve training on datasets where text pairs are labeled as either similar (both human-written or both AI-generated) or dissimilar (one human-written, one AI-generated). Recently proposed methods like CoCo (Liu et al., 2022), ConDA (Bhattacharjee et al., 2023) and EAGLE (Bhattacharjee, Moraffah, Garland, & Liu, 2024) exemplify this approach.

To demonstrate how training-based methods works, we take RADAR (Hu, Chen, and Ho 2023), an adversarial implementation, as an example and walkthrough its major training and testing steps to facilitate understanding the key ingredients. For an online demo of the trained RADAR detectors, visit https://radar.vizhub.ai.

1. Start with importing the mandatory libraries as usual.

```
import torch
from transformers import GPT2LMHeadModel, GPT2Tokenizer,
T5ForConditionalGeneration, T5Tokenizer,
RobertaForSequenceClassification, RobertaTokenizer
```

2. Initialize the models and tokenizers for two language models:
   a) A target language model, GPT2 (Radford et al., 2019), for generating texts to be detected;
   b) A paraphrase model, T5-small (Raffel et al., 2020), for building challenging adversarial training texts.

```
tokenizer_gpt2 = GPT2Tokenizer.from_pretrained('gpt2')
model_gpt2 = GPT2LMHeadModel.from_pretrained('gpt2')
tokenizer_t5 = T5Tokenizer.from_pretrained('t5-small')
model_t5 = T5ForConditionalGeneration.from_pretrained(
  't5-small'
)
```

3. Next, we need to load a human-text corpus from specific data files, but for simplicity, we use two inline text strings.

```
human_texts = ["Human text 1.", "Human text 2."]
```

4. We generate AI-text from human-texts using the GPT2 target language model.

```
inputs = [tokenizer_gpt2.encode(text, return_tensors='pt')
for text in human_texts]
outputs = [model_gpt2.generate(inp, max_length=50)
  for inp in inputs
]
ai_texts = [tokenizer_gpt2.decode(
  out[0], skip_special_tokens=True) for out in outputs
]
```

5. Paraphrase the AI-text using the T5-small model. Note that the paraphrasing prompt can be much more sophisticated than "paraphrase":.

```
inputs_para = [tokenizer_t5.encode("paraphrase: " + text,
return_tensors='pt') for text in ai_texts]
outputs_para = [model_t5.generate(inp, max_length=50) for
inp in inputs_para]
paraphrased_texts = [tokenizer_t5.decode(out[0],
skip_special_tokens=True) for out in outputs_para]
```

6. We combine human-text, AI-text, and paraphrased AI-text to prepare the training data for the detector.

```
texts = human_texts + ai_texts + paraphrased_texts
labels = [0]*len(human_texts) + [1]*(len(ai_texts) +
len(paraphrased_texts))
```

7. RADAR fine-tunes a pre-trained RoBERTa, hence we initialize the RoBERTa model and tokenizer.

```
tokenizer_roberta =
RobertaTokenizer.from_pretrained('roberta-base')
model_roberta =
RobertaForSequenceClassification.from_pretrained('roberta-
base', num_labels=2)
```

8. Prepare the input, label and AdamW optimizer (Loshchilov and Hutter, 2019), where the optimizer defines a mathematical strategy to adjust the model's weights during training to reduce errors and improve performance.

```
inputs = tokenizer_roberta(texts, return_tensors='pt',
padding=True, truncation=True, max_length=512)
labels = torch.tensor(labels)
optimizer = torch.optim.AdamW(model_roberta.parameters())
```

9. Kick-off the procedure of training the RoBERTa-based detector for 3 epochs (i.e., going through the entire training dataset 3 times).

```
model_roberta.train()
for epoch in range(3):
    outputs = model_roberta(**inputs, labels=labels)
    loss = outputs.loss
    loss.backward()
    optimizer.step()
    optimizer.zero_grad()
```

10. Once training is complete, the trained model (`model_roberta`) can be used to detect any text with an unknown source. We directly print the detection results.

```
test_texts = ["A text with unknown source."]
test_inputs = tokenizer_roberta(test_texts,
return_tensors='pt', padding=True, truncation=True)
model_roberta.eval()
with torch.no_grad():
  logits = model_roberta(**test_inputs).logits
  print(torch.softmax(logits, dim=1)[:, 1].cpu().numpy())
```

Training-based methods, despite their reported effectiveness in many scenarios, encounter several challenges such as overfitting (Sarvazyan et al., 2023). *Overfitting* often occurs when a model learns the specific patterns of the training data too well, resulting in poor performance on new, unseen data. For example, a detector trained on texts from GPT-2, may struggle when tasked with discerning texts generated from GPT-4. This problem becomes prominent when the training datasets do not cover a wide variety of text styles or domains. However, acquiring large-scale diversified (labeled) datasets covering all possible scenarios is impractical, leading to a *data scarcity* problem. Data scarcity is particularly severe in low-resource settings such as insufficient training corpus from non-native speakers (Liang et al., 2023).

Training-based methods can also be *vulnerable to adversarial attacks,* where subtle modifications to AI-generated text can deceive detectors while appearing unchanged to human readers (Shi et al., 2024). These evasion techniques include obfuscation, word permutation, and the introduction of irrelevant content (Alzantot et al., 2018). Additionally, detecting *hybrid texts,* where AI and human-written segments are interwoven, presents another layer of complexity. The subtle transitions between human and AI-generated text require deep contextual understanding and sophisticated modeling techniques to accurately differentiate between the two (Schaaff, Schlippe, and Mindner, 2023).

Watermarking techniques: sign your text

Imagine signing a mysterious manuscript with invisible ink that, when revealed, unveils the true author of the text. Similarly, watermarking techniques for detecting AI-generated texts involve embedding unique patterns or signatures into the text to ensure its traceability and verify its origin. These methods, originally developed for images, have been adapted to text generated by LLMs. Watermarking serves to protect intellectual property, verify data ownership, and track unauthorized use of AI-generated content. Watermarking could be applied to LLM training text (data watermarking), LLM itself (model watermarking), and LLM output text (post-processing watermarking). Data watermarking is a black-box technique that involves embedding unique phrases, such as "**nebula murmur tango**", into a small portion of the training dataset. LLMs trained on this watermarked dataset exhibit distinct reactions when seeing these phrases in their input, effectively indicating the use of the specific training data. As such, data watermarking mostly aims to protect LLMs from unauthorized fine-tuning or dataset misuse, rather than distinguishing between machine and human generated texts. Therefore, it falls outside the scope of this chapter.

Model watermarking embeds watermarks directly into the LLMs by manipulating the chance of outputting each word in the vocabulary. Kirchenbauer et al. (2023) proposed a method that randomly withholds a small portion of words during each step of word generation, making the resulting word distribution detectable through statistical analysis. This approach largely preserves text quality and does not require access to the model's API or parameters during detection. However, in instances where a specific word is highly predictable, such as completing the phrase "It's so simple! A piece of …," withholding the word "cake" can significantly degrade the text quality. To address this issue, Lee et al. (2023) developed SWEET, which selectively elevates the probability of withheld words in such contexts to maintain text quality. Later, Christ et al. (2024) introduced undetectable watermarks that remain imperceptible without knowing the secret key, ensuring no degradation in text quality. It has been shown (e.g., Sadasivan et al., 2024) that synonym substitution and paraphrasing can be utilized to attack these approaches; as a result, many recent model watermarking approaches, such as (Liu et al., 2024), (Kuditipudi et al., 2023) and (Hou et al., 2023) focus on enhancing the robustness to those attacks.

Post-processing watermarking is about injecting a watermark into text after it has been generated by LLMs. This technique typically operates as an independent module that works alongside the generative model's output. Early methods relied on inserting or substituting special Unicode characters, such as replacing regular whitespaces with other invisible whitespace characters, as demonstrated by Easymark (Rizzo, Bertini, and Montesi 2016). Synonym substitution also plays a role in post-processing watermarking. Topkara et al. (2006) introduced a technique using Wordnet (Miller, 1995) to replace words with contextually relevant synonyms. To automate word replacement, Abdelnabi and Fritz (2021) proposed AWT (Adversarial Watermark Transformer) that trains an encoder-decoder network in an adversarial manner to ensure indistinguishability between watermarked and non-watermarked text. Building on this, Zhang et al. (2023) developed an approach that adopts binary signatures, claimed to robustly resist various watermark removal attacks.

Now, let's run through the model-watermarking method proposed by Kirchenbauer et al. (2023):

1. Install the required package from the GitHub repository.

```
$ pip install git+https://github.com/jwkirchenbauer/lm-watermarking.git
```

2. We begin by setting up the environment and importing the necessary libraries.

```
import torch
from transformers import AutoTokenizer,
AutoModelForSeq2SeqLM, LogitsProcessorList
from watermark_processor import WatermarkLogitsProcessor,
WatermarkDetector
```

3. We load a selected pre-trained LLM, `facebook/opt-6.7b` (Zhang et al., 2022), together with its corresponding tokenizer to generate non-watermarked and watermarked texts.

```
model_name = "facebook/opt-6.7b"
tokenizer = AutoTokenizer.from_pretrained(model_name)
model = AutoModelForSeq2SeqLM.from_pretrained(model_name)
model.eval()
```

4. We also need to define the input prompt text to the selected LLM.

```
input_text = "Dr. Capy Cosmos, a capybara unlike any other,
astounded the scientific community with his groundbreaking
research in astrophysics. He is"
```

5. We first generate non-watermarked text.

```
input_ids = tokenizer(
   input_text, return_tensors="pt").input_ids
text_without_watermark = tokenizer.decode(
   model.generate(input_ids, max_new_tokens=200)[0],
   skip_special_tokens=True)
```

6. Define the watermark processor with the `WatermarkLogitsProcessor` class. Among the parameters, *gamma* is the fraction of the vocabulary to be considered as the allowed/preferred; *delta* indicates the intensity of bias in selecting the preferred words.

```
watermark_processor = WatermarkLogitsProcessor(
   vocab=list(tokenizer.get_vocab().values()),
   gamma=0.25, delta=2.0, seeding_scheme="selfhash",
   select_green_tokens=True)
```

7. Generate the watermarked text using the watermark processor defined in the previous step.

```
output_ids = model.generate(input_ids, max_new_tokens=200,
   logits_processor=LogitsProcessorList(
     [watermark_processor]
))
text_with_watermark = tokenizer.decode(
   output_ids[0], skip_special_tokens=True)
```

8. Define the watermark detector from the `WatermarkDetector` class. . Note that the values of parameters should match the ones previously set for `watermark_processor`.

```
watermark_detector = WatermarkDetector(
  vocab=list(tokenizer.get_vocab().values()),
  gamma=0.25, seeding_scheme="selfhash", normalizers=[],
  tokenizer=tokenizer)
```

9. Perform detection on the non-watermarked text and print the results.

```
print(watermark_detector.detect(text_without_watermark))
```

The visualization below highlights the detected words, with dark green indicating the preferred words.

fin **an** cially beneficial **in** America , but the **limited life of** cap y bara **allows his** body to colon **ize** Texas , but **is still mostly dependent** on paper . **Cosmos developed** a **new** enzyme that can **help** keep the micro **be in** health . R agin ' Jack is a contributing writer for the **Institute** for Astron **omy** , and a media **veteran** for the **Observer . He is** a **graduate of** the University **of** Chicago 's Albert - **Ox** ley **Research Institute** , and has **spent** most **of his career in** research and marketing . Dr . R agin ' Jack 's research **reflects** Jack 's dedication to science and **his commitment** to **promoting innovation in** our nation 's space **program . He is** a **bot** any enthusiast , **cos mon** aut , astronomical **expert , mathematician ,** electrical **engineer ,** and bi ologist . **For more information** about Dr . R agin ' Jack and to request a portrait , visit **http :// www . air in . com . Marc Gat lin is** an **editor** and contributing writer for the **Observer** . **This website was created** for public **benefit .** Dr . **Gat lin** has **authored** over 12 books on **planetary sciences ,** including **The Science of** Vir al **Sh** apes , **The Cold Current , The Apocalypse ,** and Mankind 's Secret History . **He has authored multiple** scientific novels and sym pos ia . Dr . **Gat lin also** writes about science **education** and research . To **subscribe** for the online **edition of** the **Observer ,** visit http ://**www . air in . com / sub** scribe /. **This file** uses **Creative** Commons **licensing** for all **free use** and no patents granted .

Figure 1.1. The detection result of non-watermarked text: less use of preferred words.

10. Perform detection on the watermarked text and print the results.

```
print(watermark_detector.detect(text_with_watermark))
```

A similar visualization is shown below, and we can clearly see there are significantly more preferred (dark green) words in the watermarked text than the non-watermarked text generated from the same LLM prompt.

19

> " " an expert in getting light off atoms , molecules , or minerals , " " says Gene Levin , president of the Institute of Aer on aut ics at the University of Arizona . Dr . Cosmos ' ' observation of many of nature ' ' s chemical forces , he says , has helped us pinpoint where atoms were found — on rocks , in soil , in air . But whether or not someone found something simply in the air , or in some rocks , he did , he was always trying to find new ways of measuring them . But , in his new study , he found something important . It found . For the first time , he is using light microsc opy in his brain to detect the presence of chemicals . " " Now , I am going to use them , " " he says . " " And these tiny tiny light - em itting cells in my brain — if I look like this , I will not die . " " (Er in Koch is a freelance reporter . Reach her via email : eco ch ider @ b arr ons . com) Dr . Cosmos also released a video explaining his new findings . S UR PR ISE : Is studying chemical reactions difficult ? Rec alling what happened in his latest video , Dr . Cosmos , professor of physics , asks whether he is sacrificing any of his job creation or even human civilization in his latest experiment . He notes that chemical reactions are made in single - tube glasses (those glasses made of copper or gold), but he doesn ' ' t

Figure 1.2. The detection result of watermarked text: more use of preferred words.

Watermarking techniques come with some challenges that hinder their effectiveness and widespread adoption. The main issue is its *reliance on the willingness of LLM producers to embed watermarks*. This dependency means that unless there is an enforced regulatory framework mandating watermarking, not all LLMs will be watermarked. As training and deploying open source LLMs become increasingly accessible, many models may bypass watermarking altogether, rendering this detection method less feasible in many scenarios.

As briefly mentioned earlier, the vulnerability of watermarking methods to *paraphrasing attacks* poses another critical problem. Sophisticated paraphrasing techniques can disrupt the watermark, significantly reducing the true positive rate of detection. Besides, *false positives and negatives* also present a delicate trade-off in watermarking. Enhancing a detector's robustness to avoid false positives, where human-generated text is mistakenly flagged as AI-generated, often increases the likelihood of false negatives, where AI-generated text goes undetected. This trade-off is important, as it can lead to misidentifications that damage the credibility of detection systems and erode trust in their effectiveness.

In cases where LLMs are expected to generate more deterministic outputs, watermarking is less effective because embedding a watermark without noticeably altering the text quality becomes exceedingly difficult. *Quality degradation* is a related concern; altering the token distribution to embed a watermark can result in less coherent or natural text, negatively impacting the user experience.

Additionally, *spoofing attacks*, where attackers generate human-like text that falsely triggers detection as AI-generated, pose a threat to the integrity of watermarking techniques. *Privacy concerns* arise when watermarking involves storing user-LLM interactions for future reference (Sadasivan et al., 2023), potentially exposing sensitive information. The *lack of generalization* across different LLMs and domains further limits the applicability of watermarking, as methods effective on one LLM might not work on another. Finally, the *computational complexity* involved in embedding and detecting watermarks can make these methods less feasible for large-scale applications.

While each of the detection methods discussed so far brings valuable tools to the detection of AI-generated content, they are not without their vulnerabilities. In the next section, we will explore strategies that can help overcome these vulnerabilities and enhance the robustness of AI-generated text detection systems.

Strategies to overcome vulnerabilities in AI-generated text detection

We have discussed challenges and vulnerabilities of detection methods across various categories. To combat these vulnerabilities, three main strategies have emerged: retrieval-based approaches, which leverage databases to combat paraphrased text; hybrid and ensemble methods, which combine multiple detection techniques for enhanced collective decision; and human-assisted approaches, which utilize human intuition and expertise to identify subtle discrepancies that automated systems might neglect.

Retrieval-based approaches: combat paraphrasing

Paraphrasing attacks, which alter AI-generated text while preserving its semantic meaning, significantly reduce the effectiveness of detectors in all previously introduced categories. Retrieval-based approaches address this by storing all LLM outputs in a database and using semantic similarity measures to detect paraphrased text. This method, which has shown to detect 80% to 97% of paraphrased texts with low false positive rates (Krishna et al., 2023), relies on comparing candidate texts against the database to find matches. While effective, it depends on maintaining large, comprehensive databases and raises privacy and resource concerns. Despite these challenges, retrieval-based methods provide a scalable and robust solution for detecting paraphrased AI-generated content.

Hybrid and ensemble approaches: the power of combination

To improve the accuracy and robustness of detection systems, ensembling is applied to combine outputs from various detection models. Ong and Quek (2023) demonstrated that applying ensemble methods to model-agnostic machine-generated text detection significantly enhances performance. They extended the DetectGPT model by ensembling outputs from multiple sub-models, each assuming different base models. This approach effectively integrates the diverse strengths of individual detectors, leading to a more robust detection system that can generalize across different LLMs and domains.

Hybrid detection models, on the other hand, blend various detection techniques (instead of only outputs) within a single framework, incorporating elements such as linguistic statistics, watermarking, and trained classifiers. This integration allows hybrid models to address the detection problem from multiple angles simultaneously. For instance, Zhang et al. (2020) emphasized that hybrid models could enhance detection by combining stylometric features with neural network classifiers, capturing both the shallow and deep semantic characteristics of texts.

While hybrid models integrate multiple basic methods (or components of them) into a single cohesive framework, ensemble methods combine the outputs of these basic methods to reach a consensus collective decision. Both strategies encounter challenges, such as the need for diverse and often large datasets for training, as well as the computational complexity involved in maintaining and updating multiple models. As a result, ensuring the diversity of the ensemble and balancing the trade-off between accuracy and computational efficiency are critical directions for future research.

Human-assisted approaches: letting "I" have a say

As LLMs continue to evolve and produce increasingly sophisticated text, human-assisted methods for detecting AI-generated content have gained attention. These approaches leverage the unique capabilities of human cognition and perception to identify subtle discrepancies that automated systems might miss. It is generally believed that humans possess an intuitive grasp of context and coherence, allowing them to discern patterns and anomalies in text that can signal AI involvement (Tang, Chuang, & Hu, 2024). Human reviewers have demonstrated an ability to identify certain indicators of AI-generated text, such as a lack of emotional depth and coherence (Dugan et al., 2023). LLMs, while proficient in generating grammatically correct and stylistically consistent text, often fall short in capturing the nuanced expression of human emotions and subjective experiences. This is particularly evident in contexts requiring personal anecdotes or detailed storytelling, where the AI's output may appear flat or overly formal compared to human-authored content (Ippolito, Duckworth & Eck, 2020).

However, human judgment alone is not foolproof. Studies have shown that even skilled human raters struggle to reliably differentiate between human-written and machine-generated texts, especially as LLMs become more advanced (Valiaiev, 2023). To enhance human detection capabilities, Gehrmann, Strobelt, and Rush (2019) proposed GLTR tool that uses color-coded highlights to visualize the likelihood of each word from LLMs, aiding human reviewers in spotting machine-generated text patterns. However, the effectiveness of human reviewers varies, and their accuracy can decline without proper training or familiarity with AI-generated content (Dugan et al., 2023).

The following figure (Figure 1.3) demonstrates a visualization from GLTR, which highlights the likelihood of each word being generated by an LLM, aiding human reviewers in detecting patterns that may indicate AI-generated text.

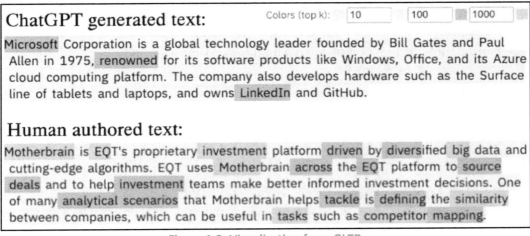

Figure 1.3. Visualization from GLTR

Green words are among the top 10 LLM preferred words; yellow words are among top 100; red words are top 1000; and purple words are "surprises" to LLMs. There is a notable difference between the human and ChatGPT authored texts. The human written text is obtained from https://motherbrain.ai.

Incorporating human input in a structured manner can significantly improve detection outcomes by combining human expertise with machine intelligence. Unlike unstructured and qualitative tools like GLTR, structured methods, such as Scarecrow (Dou et al., 2022), guide reviewers through a detailed annotation and evaluation process, ensuring consistent and thorough reviews. The structured approaches tend to enhance detection accuracy and address the limitations of human-assisted detectors. However, challenges remain in scaling these methods across large datasets, which can be resource-intensive and require costly continuous training for human reviewers.

Ultimately, the interplay between human intuition and machine precision presents a hope to develop more robust and reliable detection systems that maintain the integrity of digital content. As LLMs continue to evolve, the role of human reviewers, supported by advanced tools and frameworks, will remain crucial in safeguarding the authenticity of textual information in various domains.

A glance of public and commercial tools

At the time of writing this chapter, the landscape of detecting AI-generated text is rapidly evolving. This section provides a high-level overview of some public and commercial tools, focusing on their main features and applications.

Public open-source tools

The following public open-source tools offer accessible solutions for detecting AI-generated text, each with unique features designed to aid in identifying machine-generated content.

- **GLTR** (Gehrmann, Strobelt, and Rush, 2019) http://gltr.io
  Developed by the MIT-IBM Watson AI Lab and Harvard NLP, GLTR visually shows the likelihood of each word appearing in the context of LLM (GPT-2) generation. By highlighting words with different colors based on their likelihood, GLTR helps

human evaluators spot text that appears natural but may be machine generated.

- **RADAR** (Hu, Chen, and Ho 2023) https://radar.vizhub.ai
  RADAR trains a detection model in an adversarial manner, with one part of the system learning to create tricky AI-generated text and the other learning to detect it. This tool was developed by researchers from The Chinese University of Hong Kong (CUHK) and IBM.

- **Fast-DetectGPT** (Bao et al., 2024) http://region-9.autodl.pro:21504
  An evolution of DetectGPT, this white-box statistical model slightly alters candidate text and observes how the LLM's output probabilities change, enhancing its detection capabilities.

- **GPTZero** (Tian et al., 2024) https://gptzero.me
  Initially an academic project, GPTZero has evolved into a commercial platform designed to identify AI-generated content from models like ChatGPT and GPT-4. It provides detailed analysis and interpretability, making it useful for educators, students, and professionals.

Commercial platforms and services

The following platforms and services provide commercial solutions for detecting AI-generated content, offering a range of features tailored to different user needs, from plagiarism detection to workflow automation.

- **TraceGPT** https://plagiarismcheck.org/ai-detector
  TraceGPT features a plagiarism checker, authorship verification tool, and Chrome extension.

- **Winston AI** https://gowinston.ai
  Known for its integration capabilities, Winston AI offers tools like a plagiarism checker, readability score, and OCR for scanning documents. It integrates with various educational platforms for workflow automation.

- **Hive** https://hivemoderation.com/ai-generated-content-detection
  Hive is free and particularly noted for its ease of use and detection accuracy.

- **Originality.ai** https://originality.ai
  Catering to content publishers and agencies, Originality.ai offers different detection models based on risk tolerance. Features include a plagiarism checker, readability analysis, and an API for integration into various tech stacks.

- **Smodin** https://smodin.io/ai-content-detector
  Smodin provides a suite of writing tools, including an AI-text detector. It is known for its affordability and unlimited use plans.

- **Copyleaks** https://copyleaks.com
  Known for its robust AI content detection and plagiarism checking capabilities, Copyleaks is widely used in educational and professional settings.

- **Scribbr** https://scribbr.com/ai-detector
  Scribbr helps students and educators identify AI-generated textual content in academic writing, ensuring the integrity of submissions.

- **Phrasly** https://phrasly.ai
  Phrasly offers AI-text detection and humanization features, making it easy to ensure that writing maintains a genuine human touch.

- **Undetectable AI** https://undetectable.ai
  This tool focuses on uncovering AI-generated text using algorithms that are ideal for bloggers, marketers, and academic professionals.

- **ZeroGPT** https://www.zerogpt.com
  ZeroGPT provides straightforward scoring for quick detection and easy understanding of the results.

- **ContentAtScale** https://contentatscale.ai
  ContentAtScale offers a dual-purpose solution integrating AI detection with content enhancement capabilities.

- **StealthGPT** https://www.stealthgpt.ai
  It's primarily designed for writing and humanizing AI-generated papers, reports, and blogs to bypass AI detection. However, it also includes an AI detection tool.

- **GPTradar** https://gptradar.com
  It uses sophisticated algorithms to ensure compliance with Google's guidelines, based on OpenAI's GPT-3.

- **Draft & Goal** https://detector.dng.ai
  It offers free AI-text detection with probability scoring and supports content in English and French.

- **Kazan SEO** https://kazanseo.com
  It provides AI text detection along with several SEO (Search Engine Optimization) and keyword optimization tools.

- **Sapling.ai** https://sapling.ai/ai-content-detector
  Sapling.ai offers AI text identification with a focus of detection accuracy; it also has API integration support.

- **Crossplag** https://crossplag.com/ai-content-detector
  Crossplag detects the source of any text accurately.

- **GPTKit** https://gptkit.ai
  GPTKit uses six different automated detection algorithms for improved accuracy in verifying the authenticity of text-based content.

- **ParaphrasingTool.ai** https://paraphrasingtool.ai
  This tool identifies text generated by AI and offers an AI content bypass tool for text optimization and AI-powered paraphrasing.

- **Percent Human** https://percenthuman.app
  It offers a browser extension that integrates seamlessly with platforms like Google Docs and Google Classroom.

- **On-Page.ai** https://on-page.ai
  They provide detailed AI detection report dashboards, giving their users a quick view of AI presence reports on the scanned documents and pages.

- **Hugging Face** https://huggingface.co/spaces/openai/openai-detector
  Hugging Face offers NLP models for various tasks, including AI content detection (e.g., OpenAI Detector), with customized fine-tuning for better results.

- **Writer.com** https://writer.com/ai-content-detector
  They offer comprehensive writing services, including AI text detection, support for writing, and plagiarism detection.

- **DetectGPT** https://detectgpt.com
  DetectGPT focuses on identifying text generated by GPT models.

- **QuillBot** https://quillbot.com/ai-content-detector
  QuillBot offers a range of writing tools, including an AI content detector. It is known for its ease of use and integration with other writing tools.

- **Surfer SEO AI Content Detector** https://surferseo.com/ai-content-detector
  This free tool helps ensure the originality and authenticity of content, particularly for SEO purposes.

- **StealthWriter** https://stealthwriter.ai/detector
  StealthWriter is a general purpose detection tool to help users identify AI-generated text in various types of content.

- **Turnitin AI Writing Detection** https://www.turnitin.com
  Turnitin provides AI writing detection capabilities as part of its plagiarism detection suite, widely used in educational institutions.

- **ContentDetector.ai** https://contentdetector.ai
  It offers AI content detection services to help users ensure the originality of their text and avoid potential penalties (e.g., lower search rankings) from search engines.

While the variety of tools for detecting AI-generated text is broad, their reliability and accuracy vary significantly. Weber-Wulff et al. (2023) demonstrated that many tools struggle with misclassification, a problem that worsens when text has undergone manual editing or machine paraphrasing. This reveals significant challenges in their current capabilities. Therefore, users should employ these tools cautiously and be mindful of their limitations, especially in high-stakes environments like academia.

Summary

In this chapter, we explored the critical need for detecting AI-generated text, discussing various detection methods and the challenges posed by increasingly sophisticated LLMs. We began by examining the motivations behind detecting AI-generated content, such as combating misinformation, preserving academic and scientific integrity, and ensuring fairness in education. We then addressed strategies to enhance the robustness of detection methods, including human-assisted approaches, hybrid models, and retrieval-based techniques. Finally, we reviewed a variety of public and commercial tools currently available for detecting AI-generated text, highlighting their features, strengths, and practical applications.

In the next chapter, we will shift our focus to detecting AI-generated visual content. From images to videos, we will explore the tools and techniques available for identifying AI-generated visuals, discussing real-world applications and case studies that highlight the importance and challenges of this evolving field.

References

Valiaiev, D. (2024). Detection of Machine-Generated Text: Literature Survey. arXiv preprint arXiv:2402.01642.

Yang, X., Pan, L., Zhao, X., Chen, H., Petzold, L., Wang, W. Y., & Cheng, W. (2023). A survey on detection of llms-generated content. *arXiv preprint arXiv:2310.15654*.

Wu, J., Yang, S., Zhan, R., Yuan, Y., Wong, D. F., & Chao, L. S. (2024). A survey on LLM-gernerated text detection: Necessity, methods, and future directions. *arXiv preprint arXiv:2310.14724*.

Crothers, E. N., Japkowicz, N., & Viktor, H. L. (2023). Machine-generated text: A comprehensive survey of threat models and detection methods. *IEEE Access, 11*, 70977-71002.

Tang, R., Chuang, Y. N., & Hu, X. (2024). The science of detecting llm-generated text. *Communications of the ACM, 67*(4), 50-59.

Chaka, C. (2024). Reviewing the performance of AI detection tools in differentiating between AI-generated and human-written texts: A literature and integrative hybrid review. *Journal of Applied Learning and Teaching, 7*(1).

Shumailov, I., Shumaylov, Z., Zhao, Y., & et al. (2024). AI models collapse when trained on recursively generated data. Nature, 631(755-759).

Nobel Prize Dialogue: Fact & Fiction - The Future of Democracy. (2024). Nobel Prize. Retrieved from https://www.nobelprize.org/events/nobel-prize-dialogue/brussels2024.

Ng, D. T. K., Leung, J. K. L., Chu, S. K. W., & Qiao, M. S. (2021). Conceptualizing AI literacy: An exploratory review. *Computers and Education: Artificial Intelligence*, 2, 100041.

Zhang, M., Wu, L., Yang, T., Zhu, B., & Liu, Y. (2024). Retraction notice to "The three-dimensional porous mesh structure of Cu-based metal-organic-framework - Aramid cellulose separator enhances the electrochemical performance of lithium metal anode batteries" [Surfaces and Interfaces, Volume 46, March 2024, 104081]. Surfaces and Interfaces, 46, 104550.

Zhang, Y., Ma, Y., Liu, J., Liu, X., Wang, X., & Lu, W. (2024, April). Detection Vs. Anti-detection: Is Text Generated by AI Detectable?. In the International Conference on Information (pp. 209-222). Cham: Springer Nature Switzerland.

Bhattacharjee, A., & Liu, H. (2024). Fighting fire with fire: can ChatGPT detect AI-generated text?. ACM SIGKDD Explorations Newsletter, 25(2), 14-21.

Mireshghallah, N., Mattern, J., Gao, S., Shokri, R., & Berg-Kirkpatrick, T. (2024, March). Smaller Language Models are Better Zero-shot Machine-Generated Text Detectors. In Proceedings of the 18th Conference of the European Chapter of the Association for Computational Linguistics (Volume 2: Short Papers) (pp. 278-293).

Taguchi, K., Gu, Y., & Sakurai, K. (2024). The Impact of Prompts on Zero-Shot Detection of AI-Generated Text. arXiv preprint arXiv:2403.20127.

Uchendu, A., Ma, Z., Le, T., Zhang, R., & Lee, D. (2021, November). TURINGBENCH: A Benchmark Environment for Turing Test in the Age of Neural Text Generation. In Findings of the Association for Computational Linguistics: EMNLP 2021 (pp. 2001-2016).

Zhang, S., Roller, S., Goyal, N., Artetxe, M., Chen, M., Chen, S., ... & Zettlemoyer, L. (2022). Opt: Open pre-trained transformer language models. arXiv preprint arXiv:2205.01068.

Gehrmann, S., Strobelt, H., & Rush, A. M. (2019, July). GLTR: Statistical Detection and Visualization of Generated Text. In Proceedings of the 57th Annual Meeting of the Association for Computational Linguistics: System Demonstrations (pp. 111-116).

Su, J., Zhuo, T., Wang, D., & Nakov, P. (2023, December). DetectLLM: Leveraging Log Rank Information for Zero-Shot Detection of Machine-Generated Text. In Findings of the Association for Computational Linguistics: EMNLP 2023 (pp. 12395-12412).

Mitchell, E., Lee, Y., Khazatsky, A., Manning, C. D., & Finn, C. (2023, July). DetectGPT: Zero-shot machine-generated text detection using probability curvature. In International Conference on Machine Learning (pp. 24950-24962). PMLR.

Bao, G., Zhao, Y., Teng, Z., Yang, L., & Zhang, Y. Fast-DetectGPT: Efficient Zero-Shot Detection of Machine-Generated Text via Conditional Probability Curvature. In The Twelfth International Conference on Learning Representations.

Tulchinskii, E., Kuznetsov, K., Kushnareva, L., Cherniavskii, D., Nikolenko, S., Burnaev, E., ... & Piontkovskaya, I. (2023, December). Intrinsic dimension estimation for robust detection of AI-generated texts. In Proceedings of the 37th International Conference on Neural Information Processing Systems (pp. 39257-39276).

Yang, X., Cheng, W., Wu, Y., Petzold, L. R., Wang, W. Y., & Chen, H. (2024). DNA-GPT: Divergent N-Gram Analysis for Training-Free Detection of GPT-Generated Text. In The Twelfth International Conference on Learning Representations.

Mao, C., Vondrick, C., Wang, H., & Yang, J. (2024). Raidar: generative AI Detection via Rewriting. In The Twelfth International Conference on Learning Representations.

Guo, Z., & Yu, S. (2023). AuthentiGPT: Detecting machine-generated text via black-box language models denoising. arXiv preprint arXiv:2311.07700.

Corston-Oliver, S., Gamon, M., & Brockett, C. (2001, July). A machine learning approach to the automatic evaluation of machine translation. In Proceedings of the 39th Annual Meeting of the Association for Computational Linguistics (pp. 148-155).

Hamed, A. A., & Wu, X. (2023). Improving detection of chatgpt-generated fake science using real publication text: Introducing xfakebibs a supervised-learning network algorithm. arXiv preprint arXiv:2308.11767.

Venkatraman, S., Uchendu, A., & Lee, D. (2024, June). GPT-who: An Information Density-based Machine-Generated Text Detector. In Findings of the Association for Computational Linguistics: NAACL 2024 (pp. 103-115).

Soto, R. A. R., Koch, K., Khan, A., Chen, B. Y., Bishop, M., & Andrews, N. (2024). Few-Shot Detection of Machine-Generated Text using Style Representations. In The Twelfth International Conference on Learning Representations.

Hans, A., Schwarzschild, A., Cherepanova, V., Kazemi, H., Saha, A., Goldblum, M., Geiping, J., & Goldstein, T. (2024). Spotting LLMs With Binoculars: Zero-Shot Detection of Machine-Generated Text. In Forty-first International Conference on Machine Learning.

Wu, J., Zhan, R., Wong, D. F., Yang, S., Liu, X., Chao, L. S., & Zhang, M. (2024). Who Wrote This? The Key to Zero-Shot LLM-Generated Text Detection Is GECScore. arXiv preprint arXiv:2405.04286.

Kalinichenko, L. A., Korenkov, V. V., Shirikov, V. P., Sissakian, A. N., & Sunturenko, O. V. (2003). Digital libraries: Advanced methods and technologies, digital collections. D-Lib Magazine, 9(1), 1082-9873.

Gallé, M., Rozen, J., Kruszewski, G., & Elsahar, H. (2021). Unsupervised and distributional detection of machine-generated text. arXiv preprint arXiv:2111.02878.

Shah, A., Ranka, P., Dedhia, U., Prasad, S., Muni, S., & Bhowmick, K. (2023). Detecting and Unmasking AI-Generated Texts through Explainable Artificial Intelligence using Stylistic Features. International Journal of Advanced Computer Science and Applications, 14(10).

Li, L., Wang, P., Ren, K., Sun, T., & Qiu, X. (2023). Origin tracing and detecting of LLMs. arXiv preprint arXiv:2304.14072.

Wang, P., Li, L., Ren, K., Jiang, B., Zhang, D., & Qiu, X. (2023). SeqXGPT: Sentence-level AI-generated text detection. arXiv preprint arXiv:2310.08903.

Raffel, C., Shazeer, N., Roberts, A., Lee, K., Narang, S., Matena, M., Zhou, Y., Li, W., & Liu, P. J. (2020). Exploring the limits of transfer learning with a unified text-to-text transformer. Journal of Machine Learning Research, 21(140), 1-67.

Liu, Y., Ott, M., Goyal, N., Du, J., Joshi, M., Chen, D., ... & Stoyanov, V. (2019). RoBERTa: A robustly optimized BERT pretraining approach. arXiv preprint arXiv:1907.11692.

OpenAI. (2023). New AI classifier for indicating AI-written text (offline since July 20, 2023). Retrieved from https://openai.com/index/new-ai-classifier-for-indicating-ai-written-text

Tian, Y., Chen, H., Wang, X., Bai, Z., Zhang, Q., Li, R., Xu, C., & Wang, Y. (2024). Multiscale positive-unlabeled detection of AI-generated texts. In The Twelfth International Conference on Learning Representations.

Chen, Y., Kang, H., Zhai, V., Li, L., Singh, R., & Raj, B. (2023). GPT-sentinel: Distinguishing human and ChatGPT generated content. arXiv preprint arXiv:2305.07969.

Yang, L., Jiang, F., & Li, H. (2023). Is chatgpt involved in texts? measure the polish ratio to detect chatgpt-generated text. APSIPA Transactions on Signal and Information Processing, 13(2).

He, X., Shen, X., Chen, Z., Backes, M., & Zhang, Y. (2023). Mgtbench: Benchmarking machine-generated text detection. arXiv preprint arXiv:2303.14822.

Shi, Z., Wang, Y., Yin, F., Chen, X., Chang, K. W., & Hsieh, C. J. (2024). Red teaming language model detectors with language models. Transactions of the Association for Computational Linguistics, 12, 174-189.

Hu, X., Chen, P. Y., & Ho, T. Y. (2023). RADAR: Robust ai-te

xt detection via adversarial learning. Advances in Neural Information Processing Systems, 36, 15077-15095.

Koike, R., Kaneko, M., & Okazaki, N. (2024, March). Outfox: Llm-generated essay detection through in-context learning with adversarially generated examples. In Proceedings of the AAAI Conference on Artificial Intelligence (Vol. 38, No. 19, pp. 21258-21266).

Liu, X., Zhang, Z., Wang, Y., Pu, H., Lan, Y., & Shen, C. (2022). Coco: Coherence-enhanced machine-generated text detection under data limitation with contrastive learning. arXiv preprint arXiv:2212.10341.

Bhattacharjee, A., Kumarage, T., Moraffah, R., & Liu, H. (2023, November). ConDA: Contrastive Domain Adaptation for AI-generated Text Detection. In Proceedings of the 13th International Joint Conference on Natural Language Processing and the 3rd Conference of the Asia-Pacific Chapter of the Association for Computational Linguistics (Volume 1: Long Papers) (pp. 598-610).

Zeng, Z., Liu, S., Sha, L., Li, Z., Yang, K., Liu, S., ... & Chen, G. (2024). Detecting AI-Generated Sentences in Realistic Human-AI Collaborative Hybrid Texts: Challenges, Strategies, and Insights. arXiv preprint arXiv:2403.03506.

Bhattacharjee, A., Moraffah, R., Garland, J., & Liu, H. (2024). EAGLE: A Domain Generalization Framework for AI-generated Text Detection. arXiv preprint arXiv:2403.15690.

Kumarage, T., Garland, J., Bhattacharjee, A., Trapeznikov, K., Ruston, S., & Liu, H. (2023). Stylometric detection of ai-generated text in twitter timelines. arXiv preprint arXiv:2303.03697.

Radford, A., Wu, J., Child, R., Luan, D., Amodei, D., & Sutskever, I. (2019). Language models are unsupervised multitask learners. OpenAI blog, 1(8), 9.

Raffel, C., Shazeer, N., Roberts, A., Lee, K., Narang, S., Matena, M., ... & Liu, P. J. (2020). Exploring the limits of transfer learning with a unified text-to-text transformer. Journal of machine learning research, 21(140), 1-67.

Loshchilov, I., & Hutter, F. (2019). Decoupled weight decay regularization. In International Conference on Learning Representations.

Sarvazyan, A. M., González, J. Á., Rosso, P., & Franco-Salvador, M. (2023, September). Supervised machine-generated text detectors: Family and scale matters. In International Conference of the Cross-Language Evaluation Forum for European Languages (pp. 121-132). Cham: Springer Nature Switzerland.

Liang, W., Yuksekgonul, M., Mao, Y., Wu, E., & Zou, J. (2023). GPT detectors are biased against non-native English writers. Patterns, 4(7).

Alzantot, M., Sharma, Y., Elgohary, A., Ho, B. J., Srivastava, M., & Chang, K. W. (2018). Generating Natural Language Adversarial Examples. In Proceedings of the 2018 Conference on Empirical Methods in Natural Language Processing (pp. 2890-2896).

Schaaff, K., Schlippe, T., & Mindner, L. (2023, December). Classification of Human-and AI-Generated Texts for English, French, German, and Spanish. In Proceedings of the 6th International Conference on Natural Language and Speech Processing (ICNLSP 2023) (pp. 1-10).

Kirchenbauer, J., Geiping, J., Wen, Y., Katz, J., Miers, I., & Goldstein, T. (2023, July). A watermark for large language models. In the International Conference on Machine Learning (pp. 17061-17084). PMLR.

Lee, T., Hong, S., Ahn, J., Hong, I., Lee, H., Yun, S., ... & Kim, G. (2023). Who wrote this code? watermarking for code generation. arXiv preprint arXiv:2305.15060.

Liu, A., Pan, L., Hu, X., Meng, S., & Wen, L. (2024). A semantic invariant robust watermark for large language models. In The Twelfth International Conference on Learning Representations.

Kuditipudi, R., Thickstun, J., Hashimoto, T., & Liang, P. (2023). Robust distortion-free watermarks for language models. arXiv preprint arXiv:2307.15593.

Hou, A., Zhang, J., He, T., Wang, Y., Chuang, Y. S., Wang, H., ... & Tsvetkov, Y. (2024, June). SemStamp: A Semantic Watermark with Paraphrastic Robustness for Text Generation. In Proceedings of the 2024 Conference of the North American Chapter of the Association for Computational Linguistics: Human Language Technologies (Volume 1: Long Papers) (pp. 4067-4082).

Rizzo, S. G., Bertini, F., & Montesi, D. (2016, July). Content-preserving text watermarking through unicode homoglyph substitution. In Proceedings of the 20th International Database Engineering & Applications Symposium (pp. 97-104).

Miller, G. A. (1995). WordNet: a lexical database for English. Communications of the ACM, 38(11), 39-41.

Topkara, U., Topkara, M., & Atallah, M. J. (2006, September). The hiding virtues of ambiguity: quantifiably resilient watermarking of natural language text through synonym substitutions. In Proceedings of the 8th workshop on Multimedia and security (pp. 164-174).

Sadasivan, V. S., Kumar, A., Balasubramanian, S., Wang, W., & Feizi, S. (2023). Can AI-generated text be reliably detected?. arXiv preprint arXiv:2303.11156.

Krishna, K., Song, Y., Karpinska, M., Wieting, J., & Iyyer, M. (2024). Paraphrasing evades detectors of ai-generated text, but retrieval is an effective defense. Advances in Neural Information Processing Systems, 36.

Dugan, L., Ippolito, D., Kirubarajan, A., Shi, S., & Callison-Burch, C. (2023, June). Real or fake text?: Investigating human ability to detect boundaries between human-written and machine-generated text. In Proceedings of the AAAI Conference on Artificial Intelligence (Vol. 37, No. 11, pp. 12763-12771).

Ippolito, D., Duckworth, D., & Eck, D. (2020). Automatic Detection of Generated Text is Easiest when Humans are Fooled. In Proceedings of the 58th Annual Meeting of the Association for Computational Linguistics (pp. 1808-1822).

Dou, Y., Forbes, M., Koncel-Kedziorski, R., Smith, N. A., & Choi, Y. (2022, May). Is GPT-3 Text Indistinguishable from Human Text? Scarecrow: A Framework for Scrutinizing Machine Text. In Proceedings of the 60th Annual Meeting of the Association for Computational Linguistics (Volume 1: Long Papers) (pp. 7250-7274).

Ong, I., & Quek, B. K. (2024). Applying Ensemble Methods to Model-Agnostic Machine-Generated Text Detection. arXiv preprint arXiv:2406.12570.

Zhang, Y., Sun, S., Galley, M., Chen, Y. C., Brockett, C., Gao, X., ... & Dolan, W. B. (2020, July). DIALOGPT: Large-Scale Generative Pre-training for Conversational Response Generation. In Proceedings of the 58th Annual Meeting of the Association for Computational Linguistics: System Demonstrations (pp. 270-278).

Weber-Wulff, D., Anohina-Naumeca, A., Bjelobaba, S., Foltýnek, T., Guerrero-Dib, J., Popoola, O., ... & Waddington, L. (2023). Testing of detection tools for AI-generated text. International Journal for Educational Integrity, 19(1), 26.

2

Detecting AI-Generated Visual Content

The rapid development in generative deep learning models, including Generative Adversarial Networks (GANs) (Goodfellow et al., 2014), Variational Autoencoders (VAEs) (Kingma & Welling, 2014), and diffusion models (Ho et al., 2020), have revolutionized the creation of highly realistic visual content, ranging from images to videos. While these technologies have unlocked new possibilities for creativity and innovation across industries, they have also introduced substantial risks. Synthetic visuals, often indistinguishable from authentic media, are increasingly exploited for malicious purposes such as spreading disinformation, compromising privacy, and undermining societal trust.

This chapter addresses the growing importance of detecting AI-generated visual content. It provides an overview of the motivations, methodologies, and tools that empower stakeholders to discern authentic visuals from synthetic ones. By the end of this chapter, you will gain a wide and deep understanding of the techniques and practices required to tackle the challenges posed by AI-generated visuals in real-world scenarios.

In this chapter, we will present:

- Introduction to AI-generated visual content detection.

- Techniques to detect AI-generated images.

- Catching fakes in motion: detecting AI-generated videos.

- Two examples of real-world applications of AI-generated visual detection tools.

Technical requirements

To effectively follow along with this chapter, particularly the example walkthroughs, ensure the following prerequisites are in place:

- Python 3.8 or later.

- Required Python libraries: `PyTorch`, `OpenCV`, and `NumPy`.

Prepare your environment accordingly to gain hands-on experience with AI-generated visual content detection techniques.

Introduction to AI-generated visual content detection

The advent of deep learning has revolutionized the creation of visual content, enabling the production of highly realistic AI-generated images and videos. Advanced generative models, including GANs (Goodfellow et al., 2014), VAEs (Kingma & Welling, 2014), and diffusion models (Ho et al., 2020), have powered platforms such as DALL·E-3 (Betker et al., 2023), Midjourney (Midjourney, 2024), Sora (Liu et al., 2024) and Runway (Runway, 2024). These technologies offer immense potential for creativity, accessibility, and innovation across industries.

However, the exceptional fidelity of these models also introduces significant risks. AI-generated visuals, particularly deepfakes, have been exploited to create deceptive content, impersonate individuals in compromising scenarios, and threaten privacy, reputations, and societal trust. The misuse of such tools highlights the urgent need for robust detection mechanisms to distinguish synthetic visuals from authentic ones.

In response, AI-generated visual content detection has emerged as a critical field, dedicated to ensuring the ethical and secure application of generative technologies. By addressing the challenges of forgery and misinformation, this discipline plays a vital role in safeguarding trust and integrity in the digital landscape.

Real-world examples with wide and deep impacts

During the lead-up to the November 2024 U.S. presidential elections, AI-generated images and videos were weaponized for political propaganda and satire (Beres, 2024).

While some creations were transparently humorous, others, like the example in Figure 2.1a, undermined public trust. This particular video depicted Donald Trump waving goodbye to Kamala Harris as she walked away from the White House carrying a box of flags. Although entirely fabricated, the video circulated widely online, sowing confusion and intensifying political polarization.

Another notable example involved a fake image of a Pentagon explosion (Figure 2.1b), which rapidly spread across social media platforms. This AI-generated hoax caused brief turmoil in financial markets as some investors reacted to the false claim of a catastrophic attack on U.S. defense infrastructure. The image, though later debunked, highlighted the dangerous potential of synthetic visuals to incite panic and manipulate public sentiment (Marcelo, 2023).

(a) Fake video of Trump waving goodbye to Harris.   (b) A fabricated Pentagon explosion image.

Figure 2.1. Examples of fake videos and images generated by generative deep learning models.

Such instances showcase the profound societal harm that can arise from synthetic media, including the spread of disinformation, erosion of trust, and psychological manipulation. These examples reinforce the urgency of developing robust detection mechanisms to mitigate the risks posed by AI-generated visual content.

Stakeholders and the current landscape

The detection of AI-generated visual content is critical to a wide array of stakeholders, each with distinct needs and priorities. For *governments and policymakers*, detection tools are indispensable in combating the spread of disinformation, ensuring national security, and addressing cybercrimes. Political deepfakes, like those used in election campaigns, can distort public discourse and erode democratic processes. For *content platforms and brands*, detection mechanisms safeguard intellectual property, uphold content integrity, and protect corporate reputations. Fake content can mislead consumers or damage brand trust, making reliable detection tools essential to digital ecosystems.

The *general public* is another key stakeholder, relying on these tools to shield them from manipulated media that can exploit emotions, spread false narratives, or manipulate opinions. Educators and media literacy advocates increasingly call for detection mechanisms to be accessible, empowering individuals to discern truth from fabrication in a digital world flooded with synthetic content. Furthermore, *journalists and fact-checking organizations* depend on robust detection methods to uphold their role as arbiters of truth in society.

The current detection landscape has evolved alongside the rapid advancements in generative AI technologies. Detection methods span a range of approaches, from *observation-based techniques* that identify inconsistencies in visual content to *machine learning models* trained to discern synthetic material. *Watermarking* systems, which embed identifiable markers in AI-generated visuals, add an additional layer of verification. Yet, this field remains a cat-and-mouse game. As generative models become more sophisticated, producing content that blurs the line between real and artificial, detection systems must continually adapt.

Continued research efforts in cross-domain analysis, multimodal detection, and advanced watermarking are pivotal to staying ahead of these evolving threats. Geoffrey Hinton, widely regarded as the "Godfather of AI" and a Turing Award and Nobel Prize recipient, highlighted the urgency of this challenge: "*It's becoming increasingly difficult to distinguish AI-generated content from real material, but we can address this challenge by embedding verification codes directly into content. This way, users can confirm authenticity through trusted websites*" (Deschamps, 2024).

In the upcoming two sections, we begin with techniques for identifying AI-generated images and progressing to methods for detecting AI-generated videos, emphasizing the distinct issues posed by temporal dynamics and spatial coherence.

Techniques to detect AI-generated images

To date, methods for detecting AI-generated images can be broadly categorized into three main types:

- **Observation-based approaches** focus on identifying inconsistencies or unnatural patterns introduced by the limitations of generative models (Lin et al., 2024). Indicators include physical cues, such as mismatched lighting, unnatural textures, or spatial artifacts — like distorted facial features or irregular backgrounds — that generative models may struggle to reproduce truthfully. Observation-based detection can also involve analyzing pixel-level anomalies and identifying inconsistencies.

- **Model-based detection methods** employ machine learning models trained to distinguish real from AI-generated images. They are further divided into explainable (**feature-based**) and non-explainable (**black-box**) models. Feature-based models detect specific, identifiable features, such as periodic patterns in the images' frequency domain; black-box models, frequently using deep learning classifiers, learn complex representations that separate real from AI-generated images but operate without clear interpretability, functioning effectively as black-box detectors.

- **Watermarking techniques** embed unique identifiers into AI-generated images, allowing for proactive identification. These identifiers, or watermarks, can be visible or hidden, embedded in either the image data or metadata. Advanced watermarking strategies aim to resist adversarial attacks, ensuring that AI-generated images remain traceable even if manipulated.

Each category offers distinct advantages, addressing different challenges in detecting AI-generated images. The following sections will explore these methodologies in greater detail from a practical perspective.

Observation-based approaches

Observation-based methods for detecting AI-generated images rely on identifying inconsistencies that arise from the various limitations of generative models, particularly in reproducing realistic physical and physiological details. These approaches require human examiners to discover signs of synthetic imagery by closely inspect aspects that AI models commonly fail to render with accuracy. We will demostrate some of the most notable types of signs below, with illustrative examples.

Physical violation: AI-generated images often fail to adhere to real-world physics, creating inconsistencies in elements like lighting, reflections, shadows, and object support (Borji, 2023).

- Generated images may display *artificial reflections* inconsistent with natural lighting. For instance, reflections in glasses or mirrors might appear misaligned or overly exaggerated, as seen in Figure 2.2 (a).

- *Shadows* in synthetic images may either be missing or inconsistently placed. For example, an object lit from one direction might lack a corresponding shadow or have multiple conflicting shadows, which is visually unusual. An example is illustrated in Figure 2.2 (b).

- *Objects Without Support* are another frequent error in AI imagery. For example, a generated image might show a hat floating near, but not actually attached to, any hooks on a coat hanger, as illustrated in Figure 2.2 (c).

(a) Artificial reflection   (b) Missing shadow   (c) Floating object

Figure 2.2. Examples of physical violations in AI-generated images

These physical inconsistancies are reliable indicators because they exploit AI models' occasional inability to replicate complex interplays of light and material physics in a natural, consistent manner.

Physiological Implausibilities: When AI models attempt to replicate human anatomy or facial features, subtle inconsistencies often arise that can reveal the image's synthetic origins.

- *Hand and limb*: AI-generated images frequently display irregularities in hands and limbs, such as extra or missing fingers (Figure 2.3a), oddly shaped thumbs, unnatural finger alignment, or even additional limbs.

- *Face and neck*: AI-generated faces may exhibit subtle asymmetries or unusual features, such as mismatched iris sizes, uneven pupil placement or shape (Figure 2.3b), or irregular skin textures. Additionally in Figure 2.3a, the portrait includes a woman on the right with an implausibly stretched neck.

- *Public Figure Mismatch*: For images of public figures, comparison with verified photos from trusted sources can help reveal deepfakes. For instance, deepfaked images of Pope Francis (Figure 2.3c) can be compared to official portraits (lower-right corner of Figure 2.3c) to spot discrepancies, such as differences in ear shape.

 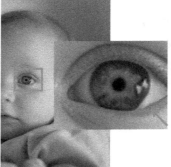 

(a) Implausible hand and neck   (b) Extra limb   (c) Public figure mismatch

Figure 2.3. Examples adapted from (Kamali et al., 2024), demonstrating physiological implausibility in AI-generated images

These physiological anomalies result from generative models having limited training data on specific body parts, which leads to misrepresentations in the final image.

Stylistic and functional artifacts: AI-generated images often display a blend of stylistic traits and functional errors that set them apart from real photographs. These artifacts may manifest as overly polished visuals, inconsistent textures, and illogical object placement or structure, revealing limitations in the AI's ability to fully replicate the intricacies of real-world appearance and functionality.

- _Plastic or glossy texture_: AI-generated portraits are sometimes unnaturally smooth or glossy, which can look waxy or overly polished, giving a plastic look-and-feel. Figure 2.4a exemplifies an AI-genrated girl (adapted from Cao, Buchner, Senane, & Yang, 2024) with waxy and cartoonish skin, yet real skin typically shows subtle imperfections, pores, and varied textures.

- _Resolution and color mismatch_: Within AI-generated images, different areas may appear with varying levels of resolution or color tone. The man in Figure 2.4b looks like he is photoshopped onto the background; and the pixels around his feet looks patchy.

- _Implausible object placement and composition_: AI models may position or align objects in ways that go againt practical logic. For instance, in Figure 2.4c, that is not quite how we eat a burger.

- _Nonfunctional or misrendered objects_: Objects in AI-generated images may lack practical functionality or appear distorted. The staircase in Figure 2.4d seems distorted and unclear where they lead to.

- _Detail anomalies_: Zooming into finer details often reveals errors, especially in textures and text. Patterns on clothing may appear warped, guitar strings misaligned, or woven objects irregular. Text within AI-generated images, as exemplified in Figure 2.4e frequently contains glitches, with letters appearing distorted, incomprehensible, or forming non-existent words. These anomalies, particularly visible upon close inspection, highlight the AI's limitations in achieving high-resolution detail, resulting in visible glitches and irregularities that hint at the image's synthetic origins.

(a) Plastic skin   (b) Resolution & color (c) obj. placement (d) Useless stairs   (e) Distorted text

Figure 2.4. Examples of stylistic and functional artifacts in AI-generated images

These stylistic and functional artifacts provide key clues to spotting AI-generated images by revealing both visual oddities and logical inconsistencies that don't align with real-world appearances. Plastic-like textures, mismatched colors, and misplaced or distorted objects highlight the AI's limited grasp of natural form and spatial logic. Detail anomalies, like distorted or incorrect patterns and texts, stand out upon close inspection, exposing where generative models fall short in replicating authentic detail.

Cultural, social or political context errors: AI-generated images may also exhibit inconsistencies that conflict with cultural norms or historical accuracy. Since generative models lack true contextual understanding, they can depict scenes or scenarios that, while visually plausible, are socially, culturally, or politically improbable.

- *Unrealistic social or political scenarios*: AI-generated images sometimes present scenes that, while appearing realistic at first glance, are improbable or misleading within a social or political context. For example, supporters of Donald Trump used AI to create images (e.g, Figure 2.5a) portraying him with groups of black voters, aiming to suggest a level of support that may not exist in reality. Such images raised serious concern around the spread of disinformation and the potential manipulation of voter perceptions ahead of the U.S. presidential election (Spring, 2024).

- *Cultural Inadequacy*: Due to limitations in the training data, AI-generated images may unintentionally violate cultural norms, especially in depictions of non-Western settings. For example, certain gestures, attire, or interpersonal interactions that may seem ordinary in one culture could appear inappropriate or unusual in another. Figure 2.5b is an AI-generated image showing Japanese business professionals hugging in a formal setting, which is atypical in Japanese professional culture.

- *Historical Inaccuracies*: AI-generated images may also include historically impossible contents. This could involve depicting historical figures in modern attire or placing people in anachronistic settings. As an example, Figure 2.5c shows a group of people in American colonial times represented by Asian girls by Meta's image generator – AXIOS (https://www.axios.com).

(a) Misleading scenario (b) Cultural Inadequacy (c) Historical inaccuracy

Figure 2.5. Examples mostly adapted from (Kamali et al., 2024), demonstrating cultural, social or political context errors in AI-generated images

These observation-based approaches enable human examiners to analyze images on multiple levels — visual, structural, cultural, and contextual — making it a comprehensive first step in identifying AI-generated content. As generative AI models evolve, some of these indicators may become more subtle; however, attention to these artifacts remains essential, as they stand for model-free and multi-dimensional means for uncovering AI-synthesized visual elements. The next section will explore model-based detection methods, which take a computational approach to this challenge by leveraging machine learning to automate and enhance the detection process.

Model-based detection methods

Model-based detection methods for AI-generated images apply machine learning frameworks to detect unique patterns in synthetic content. These methods can be broadly divided into **feature-based** and **black-box** detection methods.

Feature-based detection methods compute specific features introduced by the image generation process. These features often provide informative signatures that help distinguish synthetic images from real ones. We categorize these features into three types: *features of generation pipeline or model, features in spatial domain*, and *features in frequency domain*.

- *Features of generation pipeline or model*: Nowadays, the mainstream image generation models are GANs, VAEs and diffusion models. Those models introduce unique signatures that help distinguish the images generated from those models and the real ones as illustrated in Figure 2.6. For example, GANs often leave repeating textures due to their upsampling processes, resulting in high-frequency patterns that are especially noticeable when analyzed at a spectral level (Liu et al., 2021; Tan et al., 2024). Blending artifacts are also common in multi-task learning frameworks, especially where synthetic regions meet real ones, creating faint seams or color mismatches (Li et al., 2020; Chen et al., 2022). Diffusion models, which gradually construct images through repeated denoising steps, tend to leave distinct reconstruction patterns. Techniques such as Diffusion Reconstruction Error (DIRE) leverage these patterns, comparing original and generated versions to detect subtle inconsistencies (Wang et al., 2023; Ma et al., 2023). Together, these pipeline/model specific features can provide a foundation for detecting and analyzing synthetic images across these model types.

- *Features in spatial domain*: Natural images typically have complex, variable textures, particularly in high-detail areas, which generative models often struggle to replicate. Zhang et al. (2023) leverage inter-pixel correlations, finding that rich textures in synthetic images lack the natural fluctuations of real ones. Spatial gradients also prove useful; Nguyen et al. (2023) employ gradient analysis to detect subtle discrepancies in fine details, such as brushstrokes or shading. Another effective approach, proposed by Lorenz et al. (2023), is based on the idea that real images contain natural complexity, while AI-generated images are often simpler in structure; they calculate multiLID (multi–Local Intrinsic Dimensionality) scores from images' feature maps, detectors trained on these scores effectively distinguish between synthetic and real content, particularly for Diffusion Models.

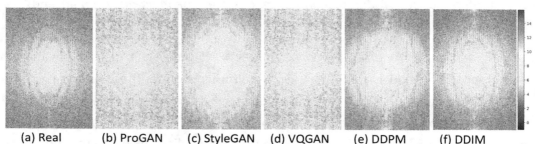

(a) Real   (b) ProGAN   (c) StyleGAN   (d) VQGAN   (e) DDPM   (f) DDIM

Figure 2.6. Frequency spectra visualization of real human face images from CelebA-HQ dataset (Karras et al., 2018) and synthetic face images created by three GAN models and two diffusion models, namely ProGAN (Karras et al., 2018), StyleGAN2 (Karras et al., 2020), VQGAN (Esser et al., 2021), DDPM (Ho et al., 2020) and DDIM (Song et al., 2021). The visualizations are adapted from (Lu & Ebrahimi, 2024).

- *Features in frequency domain*: Frequency domain features describe patterns in an image's underlying frequency levels — essentially, the rate of color or intensity changes across different areas of the image. While human eyes see pixels, frequency features try to capture how rapidly or gradually these pixels change, breaking them down into high and low-frequency components. High-frequency areas capture fine details and sharp edges, while low-frequency areas contain smoother, more gradual changes. By examining these frequencies, detectors can catch subtle, repeating textures or unnatural smoothness that generative models often leave behind. Some methods combine spatial and frequency information (Wolter et al., 2022), focusing on irregular patterns in high- and low-frequency areas, while others use tools like Fourier Transform to reveal unusual textures or periodic signals common in synthetic images (Poredi et al., 2023; Xi et al., 2023). As shown in Figure 2.6, the frequency spectra display the distribution of spatial frequencies in images generated by various GAN and diffusion models, revealing distinct patterns in texture, detail, and smoothness associated with each model. It is generally believed that frequency information helps detection tools become more reliable and resilient, especially when images are compressed or resized (Bammey, 2023).

Black-box detection methods for AI-generated images differ from feature-based approaches by focusing on *direct classification of raw images without relying on specific features* like texture patterns or model fingerprints. These methods use pre-trained classifiers (Mavali et al., 2024) or ensemble techniques (Saskoro et al., 2024) to predict authenticity based solely on image input, allowing them to operate with minimal assumptions about the generative model's internal structure. Their adaptability makes them effective across diverse generative models, including newer or unknown ones. While black-box methods emphasize simplicity by analyzing images holistically, feature-based methods employ extracted attributes, such as spatial or frequency details, which are tailored to detect artifacts from specific generation processes. This difference in input type means black-box models rely on neural networks trained on full and raw images for broad generalization, whereas feature-based models often require specific preprocessing to enhance interpretability and targeted detection. Finally, it's also worth noting that large-scale and high-quality datasets, such as (Li et al., 2024; Zhu et al., 2024), are important enablers for developing model-based detection methods.

To illustrate how model-based detection methods works, we use DIRE (Wang et al., 2023) as an example to show case how it is trained and used for detection:

11. Clone the DIRE repository and navigate into the project directory.

```
$ git clone https://github.com/ZhendongWang6/DIRE.git
$ cd DIRE
```

12. Install required packages with GPU suppport.

```
$ pip install torch==2.0.0+cu117 torchvision==0.15.1+cu117 -
f https://download.pytorch.org/whl/torch_stable.html
$ pip install -r requirements.txt
```

13. Download the LSUN-Bedroom dataset as per Wang et al. (2023) guidelines. Organize real and AI-generated images into the data folder as follows. As illustrated in the following folder structure, please ensure that the real images are stored in `0_real` and generated images in `1_fake` under both `train` and `val` directories.

```
data/
├── train/
│   ├── lsun_adm/
│   │   ├── 0_real/       # Real images for training
│   │   └── 1_fake/       # Generated images for training
├── val/
│   ├── lsun_adm/
│   │   ├── 0_real/       # Real images for validation
│   │   └── 1_fake/       # Generated images for
```

14. Initialize training components: load configuration, initialize data loader, trainer, and validation settings.

```
from utils.config import cfg
from utils.datasets import create_dataloader
from utils.trainer import Trainer
from utils.eval import get_val_cfg
from utils.earlystop import EarlyStopping

cfg.dataset_root = "data/train"
data_loader = create_dataloader(cfg)
trainer = Trainer(cfg)
val_cfg = get_val_cfg(cfg, split="val", copy=True)
early_stopping = EarlyStopping(
  patience=cfg.earlystop_epoch, delta=-0.001)
```

15. Run the training and validation loop, with checkpoints saved at the end of each epoch.

```
for epoch in range(cfg.nepoch):
    for data in data_loader:
        trainer.set_input(data)
        trainer.optimize_parameters()

    trainer.save_networks(epoch)
    val_results = validate(trainer.model, val_cfg)

    if cfg.earlystop:
        early_stopping(val_results["ACC"], trainer)
```

```
if early_stopping.early_stop:
    break
```

16. For the sake of simplicity, we will test an image in the `val` directory. Define the image path and transformation

```
import torchvision.transforms as tfs
import torchvision.transforms.functional as TF
from PIL import Image
test_image_path = "data/val/lsun_adm/1_fake/0.png"
trans = transforms.Compose([
   tfs.Resize(256), tfs.CenterCrop(224), tfs.ToTensor()])
```

17. Load, preprocess, and test a single image, then output the probability of it being synthetic.

```
img = trans(Image.open(test_image_path).convert("RGB"))
img = TF.normalize(img,
   mean=[0.485, 0.456, 0.406], std=[0.229, 0.224, 0.225])
img_tensor = img.unsqueeze(0).cuda()

with torch.no_grad():
    prob = model(img_tensor).sigmoid().item()

print(f"Probability of being synthetic: {prob:.4f}")
```

Model-based detection methods for AI-generated images face significant vulnerabilities, primarily due to their susceptibility to adversarial attacks, their limited transferability across different model types, and their struggles with increasingly realistic synthetic content. These detectors, while effective within a certain model domain, often fail to generalize when applied to images generated by unknown or emerging models (Saberi et al., 2024). Recent studies (Diao et al., 2024; Mavali et al., 2024) highlight that even state-of-the-art detectors can be easily bypassed through minimal perturbations, leading to misclassification of synthetic images as real ones. Attackers can exploit these weaknesses by subtly altering image pixels in either the spatial or frequency domain, undermining the model-based detector's effectiveness.

An illustrative example in Figure 2.7 shows AI-generated images of TEDx speakers (by https://github.com/XLabs-AI) that some model-based detectors (e.g., https://isitai.com) incorrectly classify as human-generated as shown in Figure 2.7b . Despite the synthetic nature of these images, the distorted text on the lanyards (the areas indicated with red circles in Figure 2.7a) remains a clear indicator of manipulation, which is an aspect that model-based methods often overlook. These examples pinpoint the potential benefit of integrating other detection approaches such as observation-based methods. Furthermore, model-based detectors tend to degrade in performance when images undergo compression or resizing, as is typical on social media platforms, further emphasizing their limitations in real-world and online scenarios (Yan et al., 2024; Mavali et al., 2024).

(a) AI-generated TEDx speakers by Black Forest Labs   (b) Detection results from isitai.com

Figure 2.7. Example of "perfect" AI-generated images that deceive detection systems.

These challenges highlight the need for adaptable and proactive detection methods as generative models become increasingly sophisticated. Watermarking offers a promising solution by embedding unique identifiers directly into AI-generated images, making them reliably identifiable even after modification (Saberi et al., 2024). The next section will explore how watermarking techniques enhance traceability and resilience, supporting robust AI-generated image detection.

Watermarking techniques

Watermarking techniques embed unique identifiers into synthetic images, offering traceability and enabling authenticity verification. These watermarks can be visible or hidden, allowing versatile detection mechanisms that identify and verify AI-generated imagery effectively. It can be viewed as a piece of identifiable information that is injected into an image to authenticate its source or content integrity. This process can secure digital assets, preventing unauthorized use and ensuring verifiability. The watermarking process typically consists of two main phases: *embedding* and *extraction* (Sharma et al., 2024).

1. *Embedding phase*:
   a. Watermark preparation: The watermark is prepared, often encrypted, to add a security layer. This ensures that, even if detected, the watermark remains inaccessible to unauthorized users.
   b. Watermark Insertion: The prepared watermark is embedded within the image's spatial, frequency, or hybrid domains (to be elaborated in the upcoming sections), chosen based on the desired balance between robustness and image quality.

2. *Extraction phase*:
   a. Watermark retrieval: To verify authenticity, the watermark is retrieved from the embedded image. This may require only the watermarked image (blind extraction) or both the original and watermarked images (non-blind extraction).
   b. Watermark verification: Retrieved watermark information is compared to the expected form of watermark to confirm image authenticity and trace its origin.

The primary categories for image watermarking techniques include **spatial**, **transform**, and **hybrid** domains, each offering distinct advantages based on the required robustness and image fidelity.

Spatial domain watermarking embeds unique identifiers directly within an image's pixel values, making it straightforward and computationally efficient. Early methods like Least Significant Bit (LSB) embedding (Wolfgang & Delp, 1996) use minimal pixel adjustments to encode watermarks, though these can be vulnerable to common edits like resizing or compression, which often degrade the watermark. Newer techniques in spatial watermarking build on LSB's simplicity, incorporating tamper detection and enhanced resilience. For instance, Wenyin & Shih (2011) proposed Local Binary Pattern (LBP)-based watermarking to encode patterns that better withstand light adjustments and mild transformations. More advanced methods (Raj & Shreelekshmi, 2018) use hashing or encryption, such as MD5 or SHA-256, to improve security and prevent unauthorized removal. Recent approaches, like Prasad & Pal (2020), use layered encryption techniques, further improve the detection accuracy and address tampering, making these methods especially useful for applications requiring visible, traceable marks to verify authenticity, even after minor image modifications.

Transform domain watermarking, unlike spatial domain techniques that modify individual pixel values, involves embedding a watermark within the transformed components (often "frequency coefficients") of an image. By embedding in the frequency domain, watermarking becomes more robust to common edits like compression, cropping, and scaling, as the watermark is hidden within an image's underlying structural data rather than its visible details. Techniques commonly used in this category include the Discrete Cosine Transform (DCT), Discrete Wavelet Transform (DWT), and Singular Value Decomposition (SVD), each with distinct strengths for enhancing resilience (Sharma et al., 2024).

- In *DCT*-based watermarking, an image is broken down into small patches of pixels (e.g., 8 x 8), and each patch is analyzed to find its key frequency components. Watermarks are embedded within mid-frequency values. For example, Parah et al. (2016) used DCT to achieve strong resilience against compression while preserving the image's visual quality. This approach, however, is sometimes limited in capacity due to patch size constraints.

- *DWT* divides an image into broad regions by analyzing its different "frequency bands," or levels of detail, instead of working with small patches like DCT. This allows watermarks to be embedded in parts of the image that are less noticeable to the human eye. DWT separates an image into low and high-frequency bands, where low-frequency bands hold more prominent details, and high-frequency bands contain finer details. By embedding watermarks in these less prominent bands, DWT-based methods maintain the visual quality of the image even if it undergoes strong changes, like blurring or heavy filtering (Hurrah et al., 2019).

- Unlike DCT and DWT, which rely on frequency details, *SVD* transforms an image into "singular values" that capture its core structure — focusing on shapes and patterns rather than individual pixels. Embedding a watermark in these stable singular values makes it highly resistant to changes like cropping, compression, and rotation. However, this stability is a double-edged sword: while it prevents easy removal of the watermark without quality loss, it also enables unauthorized users to recreate a similar watermark by embedding it into another copy, risking false ownership claims, which is a challenge known as the "false-positive problem" (Benrhouma et al., 2017).

Hybrid domain watermarking: Recent advancements, such as Kang et al. (2018), combine multiple transform domain methods or integrate spatial domain techniques to boost robustness, flexibility, and real-time performance. The hybrid approaches try to embed multiple watermarks to address various scenarios, such as high visibility in one layer and resilience in another. The hybrid technique is especially useful for applications requiring protection against a combination of attacks, such as adversarial or spoofing attacks, and is resilient to common image transformations like compression and noise addition (Haghighi et al., 2021)

The recent advancements in watermarking methods have shifted towards **deep learning driven watermarking**. These approaches use models like convolutional neural networks (CNNs) or GANs to embed watermarks in the "latent space", which is an underlying later where the model captures essential features of an image, like shapes, textures, etc. By embedding watermarks in this deeper latent space, the watermark becomes more resistant to alterations, making it harder for attackers to remove or tamper with it. By training on diverse image datasets, these models learn optimal embedding strategies that increase resistance to manipulations like image noise, compression, and filtering (Singh & Singh, 2024). Below, we explore two notable examples of deep learning-based watermarking methods developed by Google DeepMind and Meta.

- *SynthID* (DeepMind, 2024), a commercial tool from Google DeepMind (https://deepmind.google/technologies/synthid), embeds robust digital watermarks within AI-generated content. It is designed to ensure that watermarks remain detectable even after common transformations, such as cropping, filtering, and color adjustments. Using a deep learning-based approach, SynthID integrates watermarks without compromising image quality, embedding them subtly within the generated image while retaining resilience under various distortions.

- *Stable Signature* (Fernandez et al., 2023): Meta's *Stable Signature* is an open-source method (https://github.com/facebookresearch/stable_signature) that combines watermarking with diffusion models. Unlike post-generation watermarking, which applies the watermark after the image is created, Stable Signature embeds the watermark during the image generation process itself. A pre-trained watermark extractor can retrieve a unique binary signature from the image, which can be statistically tested to confirm AI-generated origins. The Stable Signature method achieves over 90% accuracy in identifying watermarked images even when they are cropped down to 10% of their original content.

To provide a practical understanding of watermarking techniques for detecting synthetic images, we use the DwtDctSvd method (Kang et al., 2018) to demonstrate how to embed and decode a watermark within an image. This transform domain technique combines DWT, DCT, and SVD to embed invisible watermarks. Unlike deep learning-driven watermarking, which often requires fine-tuning an image generation model, this approach allows for efficient watermarking without complex and time-consuming adjustments, making it suitable for practical, lightweight demonstration here. Readers interested in deep learning driven methods are encouraged to refer to SynthID (DeepMind, 2024) or Stable Signature (Fernandez et al., 2023) documentation for more information. The upcoming step-by-step guide will use the invisible-watermark library (https://pypi.org/project/invisible-watermark) from PyPI, which implements several image watermarking methods including DwtDctSvd.

1. Install the `invisible-watermark` library.

```
$ pip install invisible-watermark
```

2. Prepare your image: ensure the image you want to watermark is saved in the same directory as your script, e.g., `test.png`.

```
$ pip install torch==2.0.0+cu117 torchvision==0.15.1+cu117 -f https://download.pytorch.org/whl/torch_stable.html
$ pip install -r requirements.txt
```

3. Import the WatermarkEncoder and WatermarkDecoder classes from the invisible-watermark library, along with OpenCV.

```
import cv2
from imwatermark import WatermarkEncoder, WatermarkDecoder
```

4. Embed the watermark: initialize the `WatermarkEncoder`, set the watermark message (e.g., `"my_watermark"`), and embed it in the image using the DwtDctSvd method. The watermarked image will be saved into a file named `test_watermarked.png`.

```
image = cv2.imread('test.png')
encoder = WatermarkEncoder()
encoder.set_watermark('bytes', b'my_watermark')
watermarked_image = encoder.encode(image, 'dwtDctSvd')
cv2.imwrite('test_watermarked.png', watermarked_image)
```

5. Decode the watermark: Load the watermarked image, initialize the `WatermarkDecoder`, and decode the embedded watermark. The execution of the following code block will result in printing of the decoded watermark `"my_watermark"`.

```
image = cv2.imread('test_watermarked.png')
decoder = WatermarkDecoder('bytes', 32)
watermark = decoder.decode(image, 'dwtDctSvd')
print(watermark.decode('utf-8'))
```

Watermarking techniques, while effective in many scenarios, face critical limitations when it comes to detecting AI-generated images. One key challenge is that watermarking relies on the *cooperation of image-generating models to embed these identifiers*. Without such cooperation, watermarking is ineffective against unauthorized models that may entirely bypass watermarking, producing synthetic images that are undetectable (Sharma et al., 2024; Singh & Singh, 2024).

A further difficulty lies in *balancing visibility and robustness*. High-visibility watermarks, designed to withstand image transformations like compression, can visibly degrade the image, impacting user experience. On the other hand, low-visibility watermarks maintain image quality but are more easily removed through simple editing techniques. These techniques, known as removal attacks, include adding noise, adjusting pixels, or using diffusion-based models to strip watermarks with minimal visible impact on the image (Saberi et al., 2024).

Watermarking techniques also face significant risks from *adversarial attacks*, where attackers use sophisticated methods to alter images in ways that evade detection. To combat such attacks, some methods rely on high-perturbation watermarking techniques. These methods embed more noticeable modifications into images, making the watermark harder to remove or alter. Examples include Meta's Stable Signature and Google's SynthID, which aim to keep watermarks intact even after significant modifications like cropping or color changes. However, even these high-perturbation methods can be vulnerable to advanced adversarial techniques that manipulate images to obscure the watermark without visibly altering the content (DeepMind, 2024).

Lastly, *spoofing attacks* further challenge watermarking's reliability. Attackers can blend watermarked noise into real images, causing these images to be falsely flagged as synthetic. This not only disrupts detection but also risks damaging the credibility of AI model providers who rely on these watermarks for authenticity verification (Saberi et al., 2024). These limitations highlight the need for a combination of detection methods and strong defenses to enhance the reliability of watermarking in AI-generated content verification.

Catching fakes in motion: detecting AI-generated videos

AI-generated video, although visually similar in format to real footage captured by video cameras as illustrated in Figure 2.8a, is created by synthesizing frames that progress over time, capturing both spatial (x, y) and temporal (t) dimensions. The quality leap (from 2023 to 2024) in AI-generated video is humorously evident in Will Smith's spaghetti-eating example shown in Figure 2.8b. In 2023, he appears wide-eyed and bewildered, with exaggerated features giving a cartoonish effect. By 2024, however, he looks calm and realistic, naturally twirling his spaghetti, with refined textures and expressions that make the scene nearly indistinguishable from reality. This leap forward reflects improvements in mainstream video generation models like Sora (Liu et al., 2024), Runway (Runway, 2024) and Vidu (Bao et al., 2024), which primarily produce soundless videos, allowing them to focus on perfecting visual coherence and detail across frames. As AI-generated videos become increasingly realistic, detecting them is essential to prevent the spread of misinformation and protect public trust. Without effective detection, AI-generated content could be misused to manipulate perception and obscure the truth.

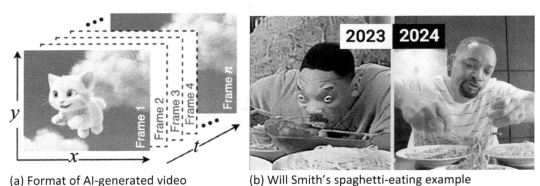

(a) Format of AI-generated video   (b) Will Smith's spaghetti-eating example

Figure 2.8. Illustration of format and fast quality advancement of AI-generated videos.

Building on the techniques used for detecting AI-generated images, detecting AI-generated videos introduces unique challenges due to the temporal dimension that must be evaluated alongside the image-based cues. While the *observation-based*, *model-based* and *watermarking methods* are still valuable for analyzing individual video frames, the detection of synthetic videos requires additional methods that account for inter-frame coherence and consistency in motion and geometry. Following most of the recent work such as (Tiwari et al., 2024; Chang et al., 2024), this section addresses the unique challenges and techniques specific to video content, largely excluding audio, for two reasons: (1) prominent video generation models such as Sora, Runway, and Vidu primarily generate silent outputs, and (2) AI-generated audio and voice detection methods will be covered in the next chapter.

Observation-based methods

Observation-based methods, fundamental to image detection, are also key in video detection. Human reviewers look for continuity in features such as color and texture, as well as coherence in spatial relationships and object trajectories across frames. Many of the visual inconsistencies observable in a sequence of synthetic image frames, such as texture irregularities or color shifts, are exacerbated in video. Human evaluators can detect these artifacts as they appear more frequently and with greater prominence across video frames. Some common indicators include:

(a) Appearance consistency: the teeth of the person get distorted across the video frames.

(b) Appearance consistency: the tattoo on the left arm of the person is changing and jittering

Figure 2.9. Examples of bservable appearance inconsistency of AI-generated videos from (a) AI FlickNips (AI FlickNips, 2024) and (b) StoryDiffusion (Zhou et al., 2024).

- **Appearance consistency**: AI video generators, particularly diffusion-based models like Stable Video Diffusion (Blattmann et al., 2023), Sora (Liu et al., 2024) and Veo (Google DeepMind, 2024), often struggle to maintain consistent appearance, color, and texture for objects across frames, leading to visible signs of forgery over time. This inconsistency results in detail such as facial features and small elements shifting subtly between frames. Figure 2.9 illustrates these issues: in (a), the person's teeth become distorted across frames, while in (b), a tattoo on the person's arm fluctuates in position, clarity and shape. These minor yet noticeable shifts, easily detected by the human eye, undermine the realism of AI-generated videos.

- **Realism in motion**: Unlike static images, videos must replicate natural motion convincingly to appear realistic. Observers can readily spot irregularities, such as jittery, abrupt, or unrealistic movements, that would be absent in real-life recordings. Figure 2.10 highlights these issues, presenting examples of unnatural motion in AI-generated videos: in (a), the runner's arms remain fixed while the legs have already switched positions in the next step, creating an awkward effect on the treadmill; in (b), the sea waves unnaturally recede from the shore, defying natural movement.

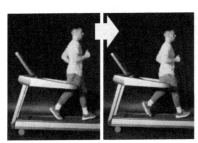   

(a) Unrealistic move on treadmill.   (b) Sea waves unnaturally receding from the shore.

Figure 2.10. Examples of unrealistic motions in Videos generated by Sora (Liu et al., 2024)

- **Geometric, spatial and causal accuracy**: For AI-generated videos to achieve realism, they must accurately capture dynamic geometric proportions, spatial relationships, and causal logic within scenes. When these elements are improperly rendered, the generated content appears artificial and unrealistic, undermining the visual coherence of the video. Figure 2.11 illustrates such common errors. In (a), a geometric error emerges dynamically as the athlete's limbs move in a distorted, anatomically implausible sequence, breaking the fluidity of natural motion and creating an awkward, inconsistent posture frame by frame. In (b), a causal error is observed in a scene where an elderly woman attempts to blow out candles, yet the flames remain unaffected, defying physical expectations. Such discrepancies, involving both physical structure and cause-effect relationships, disrupt the illusion of realism and highlight the limitations of current AI video generation models in handling complex, dynamic scenes.

(a) Geometric error in athletic movement.   (b) Candle blow fails to extinguish flames.

Figure 2.11. Examples of Geometric, spatial and causal error in Videos generated by King AI (King AI, 2024) and Sora (Liu et al., 2024)

Model-based methods

While it may seem straightforward to apply model-based methods for detecting AI-generated images (as introduced in the previous section) to each frame of a video and aggregate the results. Recent studies indicate that this naïve approach is often inefficient (Li et al., 2018) and ineffective (Vahdati et al., 2024) due to the unique challenges presented by video content. For instance, Table 9.1 demonstrates that directly applying DIRE, an image detection method proposed by Wang et al. (2023), to individual video frames achieves significantly lower performance compared to models specifically designed for video analysis. Unlike static images, videos comprise sequential frames, requiring detection methods to account for temporal changes and maintain smooth, natural transitions across frames. Model-based methods for AI-generated video detection therefore focus on evaluating temporal consistency in *appearance, motion, geometry* and *frequency* across frames to capture signs of synthetic origin.

- *Appearance*: AI-generated videos often exhibit visual inconsistencies, particularly in maintaining uniformity of color, texture, and lighting across frames. Detection models target these discrepancies by extracting high-level features from frames, using architectures like Xception (Chollet, 2017) and DINOv2 (Oquab et al., 2024). These models effectively capture subtle visual details, making them adept at identifying artifacts typical in synthetic videos, such as color gradient mismatches or unnatural textures. To assess appearance inconsistencies over the entire video sequence, mechanisms like 3D ConvNets (Chang et al., 2024) and LSTMs (Liu et al., 2024) are often employed, enabling the model to produce an overall prediction on whether a video is AI-generated.

(a) Optical flow showing motion direction.   (b) Depth map showing object distances.

Figure 2.12. Visualization of optical flow (Kuklin 2021) highlighting motion and depth information (Plank et al., 2016) revealing spatial relationships and geometry in a scene.

- *Motion*: Temporal dynamics, or the movement of objects and features across frames, are another critical aspect where generative models often falter. While real-world videos display smooth, coherent motion, synthetic videos may suffer from unnatural jittering or abrupt shifts. Detection methods, such as those by Chang et al. (2024) and Bai, Lin & Cao (2024), use optical flow analysis (Teed & Deng, 2020) to track pixel movement between frames. As illustrated in Figure

2.12a, optical flow measures the apparent motion of each pixel between two consecutive frames, creating a "map" of how pixels shift over time. This technique captures the displacement vector for each pixel, estimating motion caused by either object movement or camera shifts. By leveraging these patterns, detection models can identify inconsistencies such as jittery transitions or objects that appear to "float" without real-world momentum, which are characteristic artifacts of synthetic video content.

- *Geometric* realism in videos depends on accurate representations of spatial relationships, scale, and occlusion patterns, which generative models often struggle to maintain. Model-based detectors may leverage depth information across frames, leveraging depth estimation models like UniDepth (Piccinelli et al., 2024) and Marigold (Ke et al., 2024) to capture relative scale and occlusion cues. These models generate depth maps, as shown in Figure 2.12b, which represent the perceived distance of objects in the scene — typically, darker areas signify closer objects, while lighter areas indicate greater depth. Chang et al. (2024) utilize depth information to identify geometric inconsistencies in synthetic videos; they find AI-generated videos may exhibit objects fluctuating in size or intersecting unnaturally, defying physical constraints. Such artifacts disrupt the natural spatial coherence found in real-world content, revealing the synthetic origins of the video.

- *Frequency*: Frequency-based methods in video detection build on approaches used for images but adapt to account for the added complexity of motion and temporal changes. While image-based techniques, such as Fourier Transform, focus on static high- and low-frequency patterns to expose subtle textures or periodic signals (e.g., the DIRE method mentioned earlier), video detection expands this analysis across sequences of frames to capture evolving inconsistencies. For instance, Masi et al. (2020) introduced a two-branch network that combines spatial features with multi-band frequency analysis to identify irregularities in how patterns change over time. Similarly, Song et al. (2022) enhance detection by integrating spatial and frequency data to track texture and detail inconsistencies across frames, correcting errors caused by

62

compression or noise. In videos, these methods exploit the tendency of generative models to struggle with maintaining consistent transitions in the frequency domain. As demonstrated by (Vahdati et al., 2024), frequency-based analysis can uncover distinctive traces left by specific video generation models. By tracking how these traces evolve over time, frequency methods enhance the detection of synthetic videos, even under compression or subtle manipulations.

There is a growing trend of integrating multiple aspects into modeling procedures to create *ensemble-expert models*. For example, Chang et al. (2024) propose a pipeline combining appearance, motion, and geometry for AI video detection. As shown in Table 9.1, their ensemble model outperforms all baselines that focus on a single aspect of inter-frame consistency. Similarly, Bai et al. (2024) advocate for combining motion and appearance features, while Liu et al. (2024) explore leveraging both frequency and appearance features in their learning architecture.

Method	Input	Sora (Liu et al., 2024)	Pika (Pika, 2024)	Runway (Runway, 2024)	Average
DIRE (image detector) (Wang et al., 2023)	Image	35%	53%	53%	47%
Appearance (DINOv2 features)	Video	72%	81%	77%	77%
Motion (Optical flow features)	Video	64%	54%	54%	57%
Geometry (Depth information)	Video	80%	80%	70%	77%
Ensemble Model (Apperance + Motion + Geometry)	Video	**81%**	**83%**	**82%**	**82%**

Table 9.1. Performance (accuracy) comparison for AI-generated video detection: frame-by-frame image detection method (DIRE), appearance, motion, and geometry consistency features, and an ensemble model. Results are adopted from Chang et al. (2024).

Besides common features like appearance, motion, geometry, and frequency, *domain-specific cues* can further enhance AI video detection. For instance, *physiological signals* such as irregular mouth movements (Haliassos et al., 2021) or facial landmark (Sun et al., 2021) inconsistencies have been explored. Similarly, Qi et al. (2020) examine heartbeat signals captured in videos to detect unnatural rhythms indicative of manipulation. Another effective direction involves analyzing *audio-visual synchrony*, where exemplary models implemented (Haliassos et al., 2022) and (Feng, Chen & Owens, 2024) detect mismatches between audio and visual components. These approaches leverage the inherent difficulty of aligning human physiological and cross-modal signals in synthetic videos, offering robust detection capabilities for specific types of manipulations.

Localization in AI-generated video detection is another important research problem that strives to identify specific manipulated areas within a video. Nguyen, Fang & Stamm (2024) achieve this by generating detailed maps that highlight regions of forgery, such as spliced objects or altered backgrounds. This enables practitioners to not only detect AI-generated videos but also understand exactly where the manipulations occurred.

To offer a practical and tangible understanding of model-based methods for detecting AI-generated videos, we selected AIGVDet (Bai et al., 2024), an ensemble model, as the focus of a self-contained step-by-step guide.

1. Begin by cloning the official GitHub repository to access the necessary code and resources. Note that it is possible to skip model training entirely by jump right into step 5 after completing this step.

```
$ git clone https://github.com/multimediaFor/AIGVDet.git
$ cd AIGVDet
```

2. Download the preprocessed training and testing videos from the links provided in the GitHub repository. Extract them into the data/ directory as specified below:

```
data/
├── train
│   ├── RGB_TRAINSET/
│   │   ├── 0_real/
│   │   │   ├── video_00000/
│   │   │   │   ├── 00000.png
│   │   │   │   └── ...
│   │   │   └── ...
│   │   └── 1_fake/
│   │       ├── video_00000/
│   │       │   ├── 00000.png
│   │       │   └── ...
│   │       └── ...
│   ├── OpticalFlow_TRAINSET/
│   │   └── (same structure as above for precomputed
optical flow frames)
├── val/
│   ├── RGB_TRAINSET/
```

```
│        └── OpticalFlow_TRAINSET/
└── test/
     ├── RGB_TESTSET/
     ├── OpticalFlow_TESTSET/
```

3. Train the spatial domain detector using the raw video frames as input. This step focuses on detecting appearance-related inconsistencies. We recommend you have a default GPU available for this and the next steps.

```
$ python train.py --exp_name TRAIN_RGB_BRANCH \
    --datasets RGB_TRAINSET --datasets_test RGB_TESTSET
```

4. Train the optical flow domain detector to detect motion-related anomalies.

```
$ python train.py --exp_name TRAIN_OF_BRANCH \
    --datasets OpticalFlow_TRAINSET \
    --datasets_test OpticalFlow_TESTSET
```

5. [Optional] If you did not run through the training procedure, you can directly download the trained models from Google Drive link shared in the GitHub repository. Place the two downloaded model files in the checkpoints/ directory:

```
checkpoints/
├── optical.pth
└── original.pth
```

6. Run the detection on a single real-world video file example.mp4. The following command line processes the video frame by frame on a CPU. Specifically, the video is first split into individual frames, saved in the directory defined by --folder_original_path, and then consecutive frames are used to compute optical flow vector frames, which are stored in the directory specified by --folder_optical_flow_path.

```
$ python demo.py --path example.mp4 \
    --folder_original_path frames/example \
    --folder_optical_flow_path optical_flow/example \
    --model_optical_flow_path checkpoints/optical.pth \
    --model_original_path checkpoints/original.pth
```

7. The script outputs the prediction scores and the final decision (real or fake video). The result printouts include the Original prob, indicating the probability of the video being fake based on RGB features, the Optical prob, based on optical flow features, and the Predict, which is the final averaged probability from both.

```
Original prob: 0.85
Optical prob: 0.78
Predict: 0.815
Real video
```

Model-based methods for detecting AI-generated videos often *struggle with temporal inconsistencies,* failing to capture subtle motion anomalies like jittery or abrupt frame transitions. *Robustness* is another significant challenge, as video compression and quality loss degrade the forensic traces needed for detection, particularly in frequency-based approaches. *Generalization to new generative models* remains a persistent issue, with many detection methods overfitting to specific algorithms and failing on unseen or updated models. *Scalability* is another concern, as the computational demand of sophisticated deep learning architectures makes real-time or large-scale deployment challenging. Lastly, *limited dataset diversity* and the *increasing ability of generative models* to mimic human perception further complicate detection (Qi et al., 2020; Vahdati et al., 2024; Chang et al., 2024; Chen et al., 2024). Addressing these challenges will require robust, generalized methods that incorporate multimodal cues and account for real-world variations.

Video watermarking

Video watermarking is an essential tool for embedding unique identifiers into video content to detect and verify its authenticity, especially in the context of detecting AI-generated videos. As AI increasingly enables the creation of synthetic videos, video watermarking ensures that such content can be traced back to its origin, helping to prevent misuse and verify its legitimacy. These techniques embed invisible or visible marks within a video, making it possible to authenticate ownership or verify whether the video is generated by AI systems. This is especially valuable for content creators, media organizations, and law enforcement agencies tasked with protecting intellectual property or identifying manipulated or fake videos in sensitive contexts.

Video watermarking methods are generally classified into two main categories: **traditional** techniques and emerging **deep learning driven** approaches. Traditional methods embed watermarks in the *spatial* or *frequency* domains of individual video frames (e.g., LSB, DCT, and DWT, as previously introduced for image watermarking) or leverage temporal information across multiple frames. As an example of latter case, Bayoudh et al. (2017) utilize temporal redundancies in video frames to enhance robustness against attacks such as collusion where multiple videos are estimated to

66

remove watermarks. Deep learning-driven methods, on the other hand, employ advanced neural networks to create robust watermarks that are more resistant to tampering and transformations, such as cropping, compression, and color adjustments (Ben Jabra & Ben Farah, 2024)

Compared to image watermarking, traditional video watermarking must deal with additional challenges due to the dynamic nature of videos. For example, attacks like frame dropping, temporal compression, or collusion are unique to video content. This means that while some image watermarking techniques can be applied to videos, they often fail to withstand these video-specific attacks. Techniques like watermarking over spatio-temporal tiles or within compressed video standards (e.g., H.264) have been developed specifically to address such challenges (Gaj et al., 2017; Himeur & Boukabou, 2018). The integration of temporal and spatial information makes video watermarking more sophisticated and robust to better support for AI-generated video detection tasks.

As deep learning advances make video generation faster and more realistic, the same technology is unlocking new possibilities for advanced video watermarking methods. These approaches enhance robustness and performance, effectively "hiding the needle in the hay" to detect AI-generated videos more reliably. By leveraging neural networks, **deep learning driven video watermarking** embeds unique identifiers into the video *latent space*, a feature representation capturing the spatial and temporal dynamics of video content. Unlike traditional techniques, these adaptive methods create imperceptible watermarks that endure complex transformations, making them particularly well-suited for authenticating AI-generated videos (Ben Jabra & Ben Farah, 2024; Aberna & Agilandeeswari, 2024). We will go through some representative categories of deep learning driven watermarking methods for detecting AI-generated videos below.

Frame-based watermarking focuses on embedding watermarks into individual video frames, treating each frame as an independent image. By leveraging CNNs, these methods ensure that watermarks are robust against spatial distortions like cropping and filtering. For example, Zhang et al. (2019) employs an attention mechanism to identify regions in frames suitable for embedding watermarks, improving robustness against compression and scaling attacks. Similarly, Luo et al. (2023) uses a specialized deep learning design to embed watermarks both within individual video frames (spatial) and across the sequence of frames (temporal). It relies on a multi-level processing system and a GAN to make the watermarks strong against challenges like frames being removed or blurred.

Temporal-dimension watermarking emphasizes encoding watermarks across video sequences by exploiting temporal coherence. Unlike frame-based approaches, temporal-dimension watermarking integrates time-dependent features to ensure that watermarks remain intact even when frames are reordered, dropped, or altered. Ye et al. (2023) adapts image watermarking techniques for video by blending temporal and spatial dimensions, allowing CNNs to process sequential dependencies. This method excels against inter-frame attacks, including frame swapping and averaging.

Watermark with compression: This approach operates directly on compressed video streams, embedding watermarks during the compression process. It ensures minimal impact on computational overhead while maintaining compatibility with compression standards. For instance, Kaczyński and Piotrowski (2022) developed a method to embed watermarks directly into H.265/HEVC video files during compression. Their approach uses adjustable blocks within the video stream, ensuring the watermark remains intact even after the video undergoes heavy compression, while still maintaining clear visual quality.

Mosaic-inspired watermarking works by combining multiple video frames into a single static image, like a mosaic, and embedding the watermark into this combined image. This makes it harder for attackers to remove the watermark by averaging or manipulating individual frames. Mansour et al. (2023) introduced a version of this method that uses CNNs to embed watermarks and test their durability against attacks; and the resulting watermarks can be preserved even after video compression or changes like resizing or rotating the video.

Zero-watermarking doesn't directly embed a watermark into the video itself. Instead, it identifies unique patterns or features already present in the video frames and uses these as the "watermark." These features, which are resistant to most types of tampering, are stored separately and later compared to the video to confirm its authenticity. For example, Gao et al. (2021) used a deep learning model to extract these stable patterns from the video frames and transformed them into secure digital codes using a mathematical process called singular value decomposition (SVD). This category of methods usually provides good protection against manipulations like frame cropping, reordering, or resizing.

Baking the mark into the video's DNA: This approach weaves the watermark directly into the video during its creation, like embedding a signature into the very fabric of its design. Using generative AI models like GANs, tools such as SynthID (DeepMind, 2024) create watermarks that are invisible yet highly resilient to edits like cropping or filtering.

By integrating watermarking into the video's creation process, this method offers exceptional durability and subtlety.

REVMark (Zhang, Ni, Su & Liao, 2023) is a deep learning driven video watermarking framework that combines *temporal-dimension watermarking* and *watermark with compression* to embed invisible identifiers into videos. It uses a so-called "TAsBlock" to effectively extract the temporal-associated features on aligned frames. Additionally, a compression simulator named "DiffH264" is used to make the watermark resistant to video compression such as H.264/AVC. The training procedure aims to place watermarks in less noticeable parts of the video to keep the quality intact. Below, we guide the readers through using REVMark to embed and test video watermarks.

1. Start by cloning the repository and installing necessary dependencies.

```
$ git clone https://github.com/llcresearch/REVMark.git
$ cd REVMark
$ pip install -r requirements.txt
```

2. Download and extract the `Kinetics-400` dataset (or a video dataset you prefer).

```
$ git clone https://github.com/llcresearch/kinetics-
dataset.git
$ cd kinetics-dataset
$ bash ./k400_extractor.sh
```

3. Make sure to extract the dataset and organize videos in a folder named `dataset/raw`.

```
$ cd ../REVMark
$ ln -s ../kinetics-dataset/k600 dataset/raw
```

4. Preprocess the videos and output the processed videos to `dataset/preprocessed`.

```
$ python preprocess_videos.py --input_dir dataset/raw \
    --output_dir dataset/preprocessed
```

5. The `train.py` file provided in the repository already supports training. Run the training loop with default parameters. By the end of training procedure, the encoder and decoder models are saved as `checkpoints/revmark-encoder.pth` and `checkpoints/revmark-decoder.pth` respectively.

```
$ python train.py --dataset dataset/preprocessed
```

6. Start testing with your own video file (e.g., `sample_video.mp4`) by loading the video. GPU will be leveraged if available.

```
from custom_test import load_video
dev = "cuda" if torch.cuda.is_available() else "cpu"
raw_video = load_video("sample_video.mp4").to(dev)
```

7. Set a random watermark and embed it to the video.

```
watermark_msg = torch.randint(0,2,(1,96)).float().to(dev)
print(f"Embedded watermark message: {watermark_msg}")
```

8. Load the trained encoder and embed the watermark message to the video.

```
import torch
from REVMark import Encoder
encoder = Encoder(96, [8,128,128]).to(dev).eval()
encoder.load_state_dict(
   torch.load("checkpoints/revmark-encoder.pth"))
residual = encoder(raw_video, watermark_msg)
wm_video = (raw_video + 6.2*residual).clamp(-1,1)
```

9. Add noise to the watermarked video to test robustness in the following steps.

```
noisy_video = wm_video + torch.randn_like(wm_video) * 0.04
```

10. Load the trained decoder and extract the embedded video watermark.

```
from REVMark import Decoder
decoder = Decoder(96, [8,128,128]).to(dev).eval()
decoder.load_state_dict(
   torch.load("checkpoints/revmark-decoder.pth"))
extracted_msg = decoder(noisy_video)
print(f"Extracted watermark message: {extracted_msg}")
```

11. Compare the extracted watermark message with the original message so that we can calculate and print the accuracy of extraction.

```
accuracy = ((extracted_msg > 0.5) == (watermark_msg >
0.5)).float().mean().item()
print(f"Extraction Accuracy: {accuracy:.2%}")
```

Deep learning driven video watermarking is an emerging yet underexplored field, offering significant potential for detecting and authenticating AI-generated videos (Aberna & Agilandeeswari, 2024). Unlike traditional methods, it leverages neural networks like CNNs and GANs to embed imperceptible watermarks that remain robust against attacks such as frame dropping, temporal alterations, and compression (e.g., H.264/AVC). However, challenges like computational complexity, incompatibility with video compression, and limited benchmarks hinder its widespread adoption.

Future research should focus on multi-attack training, using pre-trained models, and exploring advanced architectures like transformers to enhance robustness and scalability. Hybrid approaches that integrate spatial and temporal dimensions with compression-aware designs could further improve performance. As video content grows in importance and regulations for synthetic media detection increase, deep learning-based video watermarking offers a promising path to secure digital content in an AI-driven era.

Two examples of real-world applications of AI-generated visual detection tools

To facilitate a tangible understanding of representative real-world use cases for tools designed to detect AI-generated videos and images, we present two scenarios leveraging a mix of commercial solutions, free-to-use tools, and open-source technologies. The first application focuses on protecting premium content, while the second addresses the challenges of detecting deepfakes during politically sensitive events such as elections. For those interested in exploring this field further, resources like the Awesome Deepfakes Detection repository (https://github.com/Daisy-Zhang/Awesome-Deepfakes-Detection) maintain a curated collection of research, tools, and datasets to deepen understanding and foster innovation.

Protecting live sports and premium content: a commercial solution

One of the growing challenges in the digital era is protecting premium content — especially in scenarios like live sports broadcasting. Picture a high-stakes championship game being live-streamed globally. While millions of subscribers watch it legally, malicious actors might intercept and re-stream the event through unauthorized platforms. This doesn't just impact revenue; it creates risks of content tampering, such as embedding misleading information or altering parts of the broadcast using AI-generated video techniques.

Industrial players, such as NexGuard™ (https://nagra.vision), addresses this challenge with forensic watermarking, embedding unique and invisible identifiers into the video feed sent to each authorized subscriber. If unauthorized streams are detected, the watermark allows investigators to trace the source back to the specific account or device responsible for the leak. This capability is particularly critical during live events, where quick identification of breaches ensures faster mitigation, reducing financial and reputational damage.

This technology is also adaptable across various types of premium content, from on-demand movies to live events, and is robust against transformations like re-encoding or scaling — techniques often used by unauthorized distributors to disguise stolen streams.

In this real-world scenario, industrial practitioners solve a dual problem: safeguarding the business model of content providers and maintaining the integrity of the original broadcast. By enabling swift identification of leaks, it helps protect the interests of legitimate viewers and broadcasters while mitigating the risks posed by AI-generated modifications to streamed video contents.

Detecting visual fakes in the year of elections: a test of tools

In the politically charged atmosphere of the 2024 election season, a video clip began to spread across social media, showing the former U.S. president Obama saying inappropriate things like *"Trump is a total and complete dipshit."* Within hours, the video had amassed millions of views, triggering waves of public outrage and news coverage.

Yet, there was one problem: the video wasn't real!

Figure 2.12. A deepfake video of President Obama: After reducing the resolution and trimming the final segment, the video was misclassified as "not a deepfake" by detection tools.

72

This scenario highlights the critical challenge of deepfake detection during elections, where false media can influence public opinion and even destabilize democratic processes. To address this, Anlen & Vázquez Llorente (2024) tested some mainstream tools for detecting AI-generated visual, including **Optic** (https://www.aiornot.com), **Hive Moderation** (https://hivemoderation.com), **V7 Labs** (https://www.v7labs.com), **Invid Verification Plugin** (https://www.invid-project.eu/tools-and-services/invid-verification-plugin), **Deepware Scanner** (https://scanner.deepware.ai), **Illuminarty** (https://app.illuminarty.ai), **DeepID** (https://deepmedia.ai) and open-source **HuggingFace AI image detector** (https://huggingface.co/umm-maybe/AI-image-detector). Each was evaluated on its ability to identify synthetic content for the 2024 U.S. presidential election, particularly deepfakes crafted with generative AI technologies like GANs and diffusion models.

The tools demonstrated varying degrees of success. For instance:

- **Hive Moderation** and **Deepware Scanner** excelled in identifying GAN-based media, such as fake profile pictures, where predictable facial features could be flagged.

- **InVid Verification Plugin** specialized in analyzing video content, offering frame-by-frame assessments for detecting temporal inconsistencies typical of deepfakes.

- **Optic** and **Illuminarty**, while user-friendly, struggled when videos were cropped, compressed, or blurred — common tactics used by malicious actors to evade detection.

A notable failure occurred with a deepfake of a well-known political figure. By simply reducing the resolution and trimming the video, even the best-performing detectors misclassified the manipulated content as real. Similarly, audio detection tools failed to identify an AI-generated political robocall once it was re-recorded and analyzed under suboptimal conditions (Anlen & Vázquez Llorente, 2024). Overall, the tests uncovered three key limitations:

- Overfitting to known patterns: Many tools are trained on specific datasets and excel at detecting synthetic content within those constraints. However, real-world scenarios often involve novel manipulations.

- Vulnerability to degradations: Compression, cropping, and scaling can significantly reduce detection accuracy. These transformations strip metadata and reduce the visible cues that detectors rely on.

- Interpretation of results: Tools often provide probabilistic outcomes (e.g., "85% likely human"). Without clear explanations of confidence levels and underlying models, users may misinterpret these results.

The limitations of the tested detection tools underscore the need for multi-faceted approaches. *Computational detection must be complemented by observation-based human expertise, reverse image searches, and provenance tracking.* Tools like Optic and Hive Moderation serve as starting points, but they are not standalone solutions. Transparency about their capabilities and limitations is essential to fostering trust and ensuring responsible usage during critical moments, such as elections.

Summary

This chapter discusses the pressing challenges and advancements in detecting AI-generated visual content, focusing on both images and videos. With the rise of sophisticated generative models like GANs, VAEs, and diffusion models, synthetic visuals have become nearly indistinguishable from authentic ones, posing risks to privacy, trust, and societal integrity. The chapter explores observation-based, model-based, and watermarking techniques as key methodologies for identifying inconsistencies and traces in AI-generated media. Real-world examples, such as deepfakes influencing political events and watermarking applications in live sports streaming, underscore the societal and industrial stakes of robust detection mechanisms. It emphasizes the need for interdisciplinary approaches combining technical innovation, human expertise, and ethical considerations to combat misuse while preserving the creative potential of AI. Through practical walkthroughs and case studies, the chapter provides a comprehensive understanding of tools and methods to detect and mitigate the impact of synthetic visual content in real-world contexts.

References

Midjourney. (2024). Retrieved November 19, 2024, from https://www.midjourney.com.

Betker, J., Goh, G., Jing, L., Brooks, T., Wang, J., Li, L., Ouyang, L., Zhuang, J., Lee, J., Guo, Y., et al. (2023). Improving image generation with better captions. *Computer Science, 2*(3), 8. Retrieved from https://openai.com/index/dall-e-3.

Beres, D. (2024, November 15). AI's fingerprints were all over the election. *The Atlantic.* https://www.theatlantic.com/technology/archive/2024/11/ai-election-propaganda/680677.

Marcelo, P. (2023, May 22). Fact focus: Fake image of Pentagon explosion briefly sends jitters through stock market. *Associated Press.* https://apnews.com/article/pentagon-explosion-misinformation-stock-market-ai-96f534c790872fde67012ee81b5ed6a4.

Deschamps, T. (2024, October 28). Fake content is getting harder to detect but Hinton has an idea to make it easier. *Times Colonist.* https://www.timescolonist.com/national-news/fake-content-is-getting-harder-to-detect-but-hinton-has-an-idea-to-make-it-easier-9723734.

Lin, L., Gupta, N., Zhang, Y., Ren, H., Liu, C.-H., Ding, F., Wang, X., Li, X., Verdoliva, L., & Hu, S. (2024). Detecting multimedia generated by large AI models: A survey. *arXiv preprint arXiv:2402.00045.*

Borji, A. (2023). Qualitative failures of image generation models and their application in detecting deepfakes. *Image and Vision Computing, 137*, 104771. Elsevier.

Kamali, N., Nakamura, K., Chatzimparmpas, A., Hullman, J., & Groh, M. (2024). How to distinguish AI-generated images from authentic photographs. *arXiv preprint arXiv:2406.08651.*

Cao, L., Buchner, V., Senane, Z., & Yang, F. (2024). Introducing GenCeption for multimodal LLM benchmarking: You may bypass annotations. *Proceedings of the 4th Workshop on Trustworthy Natural Language Processing (TrustNLP 2024)*, 196–201.

Spring, M. (2024, March 4). *Trump supporters target black voters with faked AI images.* BBC Panorama and Americast. https://www.bbc.com/news/world-us-canada-68440150.

Goodfellow, I., Pouget-Abadie, J., Mirza, M., Xu, B., Warde-Farley, D., Ozair, S., Courville, A., & Bengio, Y. (2014). Generative adversarial nets. *Advances in Neural Information Processing Systems, 27.*

Kingma, D. P., & Welling, M. (2014). Auto-encoding variational Bayes. *Proceedings of the 2nd International Conference on Learning Representations (ICLR).*

Ho, J., Jain, A., & Abbeel, P. (2020). Denoising diffusion probabilistic models. *Advances in Neural Information Processing Systems, 33*, 6840–6851.

Tan, C., Zhao, Y., Wei, S., Gu, G., Liu, P., & Wei, Y. (2024). Rethinking the up-sampling operations in CNN-based generative network for generalizable deepfake detection. *In Proceedings of the IEEE/CVF Conference on Computer Vision and Pattern Recognition*, 28130–28139.

Liu, H., Li, X., Zhou, W., Chen, Y., He, Y., Xue, H., Zhang, W., & Yu, N. (2021). Spatial-phase shallow learning: Rethinking face forgery detection in frequency domain. *In Proceedings of the IEEE/CVF Conference on Computer Vision and Pattern Recognition*, 772–781.

Li, L., Bao, J., Zhang, T., Yang, H., Chen, D., Wen, F., & Guo, B. (2020). Face x-ray for more general face forgery detection. In *Proceedings of the IEEE/CVF conference on computer vision and pattern recognition* (pp. 5001–5010).

Chen, L., Zhang, Y., Song, Y., Liu, L., & Wang, J. (2022). Self-supervised learning of adversarial example: Towards good generalizations for deepfake detection. In *Proceedings of the IEEE/CVF conference on computer vision and pattern recognition* (pp. 18710–18719).

Wang, Z., Bao, J., Zhou, W., Wang, W., Hu, H., Chen, H., & Li, H. (2023). Dire for diffusion-generated image detection. In *Proceedings of the IEEE/CVF International Conference on Computer Vision* (pp. 22445–22455).

Ma, R., Duan, J., Kong, F., Shi, X., & Xu, K. (2023). Exposing the fake: Effective diffusion-generated images detection. In *The Second Workshop on New Frontiers in Adversarial Machine Learning*.

Zhong, N., Xu, Y., Qian, Z., & Zhang, X. (2023). Rich and poor texture contrast: A simple yet effective approach for AI-generated image detection. *arXiv preprint arXiv:2311.12397*.

Nguyen, M.-Q., Ho, K.-D., Nguyen, H.-M., Tu, C.-M., Tran, M.-T., & Do, T.-L. (2023). Unmasking the artist: Discriminating human-drawn and AI-generated human face art through facial feature analysis. In *2023 International Conference on Multimedia Analysis and Pattern Recognition (MAPR)* (pp. 1–6). IEEE.

Lorenz, P., Durall, R. L., & Keuper, J. (2023). Detecting images generated by deep diffusion models using their local intrinsic dimensionality. In *Proceedings of the IEEE/CVF International Conference on Computer Vision* (pp. 448–459).

Wolter, M., Blanke, F., Heese, R., & Garcke, J. (2022). Wavelet-packets for deepfake image analysis and detection. *Machine Learning, 111*(11), 4295–4327. Springer.

Xi, Z., Huang, W., Wei, K., Luo, W., & Zheng, P. (2023). AI-generated image detection using a cross-attention enhanced dual-stream network. In *2023 Asia Pacific Signal and Information Processing Association Annual Summit and Conference (APSIPA ASC)* (pp. 1463–1470). IEEE.

Poredi, N., Nagothu, D., & Chen, Y. (2023). AUSOME: Authenticating social media images using frequency analysis. In *Disruptive Technologies in Information Sciences VII* (Vol. 12542, pp. 44–56). SPIE.

Bammey, Q. (2023). Synthbuster: Towards detection of diffusion model generated images. *IEEE Open Journal of Signal Processing*. IEEE.

Karras, T., Aila, T., Laine, S., & Lehtinen, J. (2018). Progressive growing of GANs for improved quality, stability, and variation. In *International Conference on Learning Representations*. https://github.com/tkarras/progressive_growing_of_gans.

Karras, T., Laine, S., Aittala, M., Hellsten, J., Lehtinen, J., & Aila, T. (2020). Analyzing and improving the image quality of StyleGAN. In *Proceedings of the IEEE/CVF Conference on Computer Vision and Pattern Recognition* (pp. 8110–8119).

Esser, P., Rombach, R., & Ommer, B. (2021). Taming transformers for high-resolution image synthesis. In *Proceedings of the IEEE/CVF Conference on Computer Vision and Pattern Recognition* (pp. 12873–12883).

Song, J., Meng, C., & Ermon, S. (2021). Denoising diffusion implicit models. In *International Conference on Learning Representations*.

Lu, Y., & Ebrahimi, T. (2024). Towards the detection of AI-synthesized human face images. In *2024 IEEE International Conference on Image Processing (ICIP)*.

Mavali, S., Ricker, J., Pape, D., Sharma, Y., Fischer, A., & Schönherr, L. (2024). Fake it until you break it: On the adversarial robustness of AI-generated image detectors. *arXiv preprint arXiv:2410.01574*.

Diao, Y., Zhai, N., Miao, C., Yang, X., & Wang, M. (2024). Vulnerabilities in AI-generated image detection: The challenge of adversarial attacks. *arXiv preprint arXiv:2407.20836*.

Saskoro, R. A. F., Yudistira, N., & Fatyanosa, T. N. (2024). Detection of AI-generated images from various generators using gated expert convolutional neural network. *IEEE Access*. IEEE.

Li, Y., Liu, Z., Zhao, J., Ren, L., Li, F., Luo, J., & Luo, B. (2024). The adversarial AI-art: Understanding, generation, detection, and benchmarking. In *European Symposium on Research in Computer Security* (pp. 311–331). Springer.

Zhu, M., Chen, H., Yan, Q., Huang, X., Lin, G., Li, W., Tu, Z., Hu, H., Hu, J., & Wang, Y. (2024). Genimage: A million-scale benchmark for detecting AI-generated image. *Advances in Neural Information Processing Systems, 36*.

Saberi, M., Sadasivan, V. S., Rezaei, K., Kumar, A., Chegini, A., Wang, W., & Feizi, S. (2024). Robustness of AI-image detectors: Fundamental limits and practical attacks. In *The Twelfth International Conference on Learning Representations*.

Yan, S., Li, O., Cai, J., Hao, Y., Jiang, X., Hu, Y., & Xie, W. (2024). A sanity check for AI-generated image detection. *arXiv preprint arXiv:2406.19435*.

Sharma, S., Zou, J. J., Fang, G., Shukla, P., & Cai, W. (2024). A review of image watermarking for identity protection and verification. *Multimedia Tools and Applications, 83*(11), 31829–31891. Springer.

Wolfgang, R. B., & Delp, E. J. (1996). A watermark for digital images. In *Proceedings of the 3rd IEEE International Conference on Image Processing* (Vol. 3, pp. 219–222). IEEE.

Wenyin, Z., & Shih, F. Y. (2011). Semi-fragile spatial watermarking based on local binary pattern operators. *Optics Communications, 284*(16-17), 3904–3912. Elsevier.

Raj, N. N., & Shreelekshmi, R. (2018). Blockwise fragile watermarking schemes for tamper localization in digital images. In *2018 International CET Conference on Control, Communication, and Computing (IC4)* (pp. 441–446). IEEE.

Parah, S. A., Sheikh, J. A., Loan, N. A., & Bhat, G. M. (2016). Robust and blind watermarking technique in DCT domain using inter-block coefficient differencing. *Digital Signal Processing, 53*, 11–24. Elsevier.

Hurrah, N. N., Parah, S. A., Loan, N. A., Sheikh, J. A., Elhoseny, M., & Muhammad, K. (2019). Dual watermarking framework for privacy protection and content authentication of multimedia. *Future Generation Computer Systems, 94*, 654–673. Elsevier.

Benrhouma, O., Hermassi, H., & Belghith, S. (2017). Security analysis and improvement of an active watermarking system for image tampering detection using a self-recovery scheme. *Multimedia Tools and Applications, 76*, 21133–21156. Springer.

Kang, X., Zhao, F., Lin, G., & Chen, Y. (2018). A novel hybrid of DCT and SVD in DWT domain for robust and invisible blind image watermarking with optimal embedding strength. *Multimedia Tools and Applications, 77*, 13197–13224. Springer.

Haghighi, B. B., Taherinia, A. H., Harati, A., & Rouhani, M. (2021). WSMN: An optimized multipurpose blind watermarking in Shearlet domain using MLP and NSGA-II. *Applied Soft Computing, 101*, 107029. Elsevier.

Singh, H. K., & Singh, A. K. (2024). Digital image watermarking using deep learning. *Multimedia Tools and Applications, 83*(1), 2979–2994. Springer.

Fernandez, P., Couairon, G., Jégou, H., Douze, M., & Furon, T. (2023). The stable signature: Rooting watermarks in latent diffusion models. In *Proceedings of the IEEE/CVF International Conference on Computer Vision* (pp. 22466–22477). https://github.com/facebookresearch/stable_signature.

DeepMind. (2024). SynthID. Retrieved from https://deepmind.google/technologies/synthid

Liu, Y., Zhang, K., Li, Y., Yan, Z., Gao, C., Chen, R., Yuan, Z., Huang, Y., Sun, H., Gao, J., et al. (2024). Sora: A review on background, technology, limitations, and opportunities of large vision models. *arXiv preprint arXiv:2402.17177*. https://openai.com/index/sora.

Bao, F., Xiang, C., Yue, G., He, G., Zhu, H., Zheng, K., Zhao, M., Liu, S., Wang, Y., & Zhu, J. (2024). Vidu: A highly consistent, dynamic and skilled text-to-video generator with diffusion models. *arXiv preprint arXiv:2405.04233*. https://www.vidu.studio.

Runway. (2024). Introducing Gen-3 Alpha. Retrieved November 11, 2024, from https://runwayml.com/research/introducing-gen-3-alpha.

Tiwari, A. K., Sharma, A., Rayakar, P., Bhavriya, M. K., et al. (2024). AI-generated video forgery detection and authentication. In *2024 IEEE 9th International Conference for Convergence in Technology (I2CT)* (pp. 1–8). IEEE.

Chang, C., Liu, Z., Lyu, X., & Qi, X. (2024). What matters in detecting AI-generated videos like Sora? *arXiv preprint arXiv:2406.19568*.

Zhou, Y., Zhou, D., Cheng, M.-M., Feng, J., & Hou, Q. (2024). StoryDiffusion: Consistent self-attention for long-range image and video generation. *arXiv preprint arXiv:2405.01434*. https://storydiffusion.github.io.

AI FlickNips. (2004). *AI Flick Nips* [YouTube Channel]. YouTube. Retrieved November 15, 2024, from https://www.youtube.com/@AIFlickNips.

Blattmann, A., Dockhorn, T., Kulal, S., Mendelevitch, D., Kilian, M., Lorenz, D., Levi, Y., English, Z., Voleti, V., Letts, A., et al. (2023). Stable video diffusion: Scaling latent video diffusion models to large datasets. *arXiv preprint arXiv:2311.15127*.

Google DeepMind. (2024) Veo. Retrieved November 15, 2024, from https://deepmind.google/technologies/veo.

Kling AI. (2024). Retrieved November 15, 2024, from https://www.klingai.com.

Vahdati, D. S., Nguyen, T. D., Azizpour, A., & Stamm, M. C. (2024). Beyond deepfake images: Detecting AI-generated videos. In *Proceedings of the IEEE/CVF Conference on Computer Vision and Pattern Recognition* (pp. 4397–4408).

Li, Y., Chang, M.-C., & Lyu, S. (2018). In ictu oculi: Exposing AI created fake videos by detecting eye blinking. In *2018 IEEE International Workshop on Information Forensics and Security (WIFS)* (pp. 1–7). IEEE.

Liu, Q., Shi, P., Tsai, Y.-Y., Mao, C., & Yang, J. (2024). Turns out I'm not real: Towards robust detection of AI-generated videos. *arXiv preprint arXiv:2406.09601.*

Oquab, M., Darcet, T., Moutakanni, T., Vo, H. V., Szafraniec, M., Khalidov, V., Fernandez, P., Haziza, D., Massa, F., El-Nouby, A., Assran, M., Ballas, N., Galuba, W., Howes, R., Huang, P.-Y., Li, S.-W., Misra, I., Rabbat, M., Sharma, V., Synnaeve, G., Xu, H., Jegou, H., Mairal, J., Labatut, P., Joulin, A., & Bojanowski, P. (2024). DINOv2: Learning robust visual features without supervision. *Transactions on Machine Learning Research.*

Chollet, F. (2017). Xception: Deep learning with depthwise separable convolutions. In *Proceedings of the IEEE Conference on Computer Vision and Pattern Recognition* (pp. 1251–1258).

Teed, Z., & Deng, J. (2020). RAFT: Recurrent all-pairs field transforms for optical flow. In *Computer Vision–ECCV 2020: 16th European Conference, Glasgow, UK, August 23–28, 2020, Proceedings, Part II* (pp. 402–419). Springer.

Bai, J., Lin, M., Cao, G., & Lou, Z. (2024). AI-generated video detection via spatial-temporal anomaly learning. In *The 7th Chinese Conference on Pattern Recognition and Computer Vision (PRCV).*

Ke, B., Obukhov, A., Huang, S., Metzger, N., Daudt, R. C., & Schindler, K. (2024). Repurposing diffusion-based image generators for monocular depth estimation. In *Proceedings of the IEEE/CVF Conference on Computer Vision and Pattern Recognition* (pp. 9492–9502).

Piccinelli, L., Yang, Y.-H., Sakaridis, C., Segu, M., Li, S., Van Gool, L., & Yu, F. (2024). UniDepth: Universal monocular metric depth estimation. In *Proceedings of the IEEE/CVF Conference on Computer Vision and Pattern Recognition* (pp. 10106–10116).

Masi, I., Killekar, A., Mascarenhas, R. M., Gurudatt, S. P., & AbdAlmageed, W. (2020). Two-branch recurrent network for isolating deepfakes in videos. In *Computer Vision–ECCV 2020: 16th European Conference, Glasgow, UK, August 23–28, 2020, Proceedings, Part VII* (pp. 667–684). Springer.

Song, L., Fang, Z., Li, X., Dong, X., Jin, Z., Chen, Y., & Lyu, S. (2022). Adaptive face forgery detection in cross domain. In *European Conference on Computer Vision* (pp. 467–484). Springer.

Nguyen, T. D., Fang, S., & Stamm, M. C. (2024). Videofact: Detecting video forgeries using attention, scene context, and forensic traces. In *Proceedings of the IEEE/CVF Winter Conference on Applications of Computer Vision* (pp. 8563–8573).

Haliassos, A., Vougioukas, K., Petridis, S., & Pantic, M. (2021). Lips don't lie: A generalisable and robust approach to face forgery detection. In *Proceedings of the IEEE/CVF Conference on Computer Vision and Pattern Recognition* (pp. 5039–5049).

Sun, Z., Han, Y., Hua, Z., Ruan, N., & Jia, W. (2021). Improving the efficiency and robustness of deepfakes detection through precise geometric features. In *Proceedings of the IEEE/CVF Conference on Computer Vision and Pattern Recognition* (pp. 3609–3618).

Qi, H., Guo, Q., Juefei-Xu, F., Xie, X., Ma, L., Feng, W., Liu, Y., & Zhao, J. (2020). Deeprhythm: Exposing deepfakes with attentional visual heartbeat rhythms. In *Proceedings of the 28th ACM International Conference on Multimedia* (pp. 4318–4327).

Haliassos, A., Mira, R., Petridis, S., & Pantic, M. (2022). Leveraging real talking faces via self-supervision for robust forgery detection. In *Proceedings of the IEEE/CVF Conference on Computer Vision and Pattern Recognition* (pp. 14950–14962).

Feng, C., Chen, Z., & Owens, A. (2023). Self-supervised video forensics by audio-visual anomaly detection. In *Proceedings of the IEEE/CVF Conference on Computer Vision and Pattern Recognition* (pp. 10491–10503).

Pika. (2024). Retrieved November 16, 2024, from https://pika.art.

Chen, H., Hong, Y., Huang, Z., Xu, Z., Gu, Z., Li, Y., Lan, J., Zhu, H., Zhang, J., Wang, W., & others. (2024). DeMamba: AI-generated video detection on million-scale GenVideo benchmark. *arXiv preprint arXiv:2405.19707*.

Bayoudh, I., Ben Jabra, S., & Zagrouba, E. (2017). A robust video watermarking for real-time application. In *Advanced Concepts for Intelligent Vision Systems: 18th International Conference, ACIVS 2017, Antwerp, Belgium, September 18-21, 2017, Proceedings* (pp. 493–504). Springer.

Ben Jabra, S., & Ben Farah, M. (2024). Deep learning-based watermarking techniques challenges: A review of current and future trends. *Circuits, Systems, and Signal Processing*, 1–30. Springer.

Gaj, S., Kanetkar, A., Sur, A., & Bora, P. K. (2017). Drift-compensated robust watermarking algorithm for H.265/HEVC video stream. *ACM Transactions on Multimedia Computing, Communications, and Applications (TOMM), 13*(1), 1–24. ACM.

Himeur, Y., & Boukabou, A. (2018). A robust and secure key-frames based video watermarking system using chaotic encryption. *Multimedia Tools and Applications, 77*, 8603–8627. Springer.

Aberna, P., & Agilandeeswari, L. (2024). Digital image and video watermarking: Methodologies, attacks, applications, and future directions. *Multimedia Tools and Applications, 83*(2), 5531–5591. Springer.

Zhang, K. A., Xu, L., Cuesta-Infante, A., & Veeramachaneni, K. (2019). Robust invisible video watermarking with attention. *arXiv preprint arXiv:1909.01285*.

Luo, X., Li, Y., Chang, H., Liu, C., Milanfar, P., & Yang, F. (2023). DVMark: A deep multiscale framework for video watermarking. *IEEE Transactions on Image Processing*. IEEE.

Ye, G., Gao, J., Wang, Y., Song, L., & Wei, X. (2023). ItoV: Efficiently adapting deep learning-based image watermarking to video watermarking. In *2023 International Conference on Culture-Oriented Science and Technology (CoST)* (pp. 192–197). IEEE.

Kaczyński, M., & Piotrowski, Z. (2022). High-quality video watermarking based on deep neural networks and adjustable subsquares properties algorithm. *Sensors, 22*(14), 5376. MDPI.

Mansour, S., Ben Jabra, S., & Zagrouba, E. (2023). A robust deep learning-based video watermarking using mosaic generation. In *VISIGRAPP (5: VISAPP)* (pp. 668–675).

Gao, Y., Kang, X., & Chen, Y. (2021). A robust video zero-watermarking based on deep convolutional neural network and self-organizing map in polar complex exponential transform domain. *Multimedia Tools and Applications, 80*(4), 6019–6039.

Zhang, Y., Ni, J., Su, W., & Liao, X. (2023). A novel deep video watermarking framework with enhanced robustness to H.264/AVC compression. In *Proceedings of the 31st ACM International Conference on Multimedia* (pp. 8095–8104).

Plank, H., Holweg, G., Herndl, T., & Druml, N. (2016). High performance time-of-flight and color sensor fusion with image-guided depth super resolution. In *2016 Design, Automation & Test in Europe Conference & Exhibition (DATE)* (pp. 1213–1218). IEEE.

Kuklin, M. (2021, January 4). Optical flow in OpenCV (C++/Python). *LearnOpenCV*. https://learnopencv.com/optical-flow-in-opencv.

Anlen, S., & Vázquez Llorente, R. (2024, April 15). Spotting deepfakes in a year of elections: How AI detection tools work and where they fail. *Reuters Institute*. https://reutersinstitute.politics.ox.ac.uk/news/spotting-deepfakes-year-elections-how-ai-detection-tools-work-and-where-they-fail.

3

Discerning AI-Generated Audio and Music

The emergence of advanced generative models in AI, including text-to-speech (TTS) systems, voice conversion (VC) algorithms, and AI music generation platforms, has profoundly transformed the landscape of audio and music creation. These technologies are no longer confined to research laboratories; they now power personalized voice assistants, automated music composition tools, and synthetic audio in media production. While such advancements unlock remarkable opportunities for innovation and efficiency, they also introduce significant risks. Synthetic voices are increasingly leveraged for deepfake scams and identity fraud, while AI-generated music raises concerns about originality, copyright infringement, and artistic integrity.

This chapter explores the dual-edged impact of AI-generated audio and music. It delves into the challenges of distinguishing synthetic content from authentic recordings, offering a technical and practical guide to navigating this complex field. Readers will gain a deeper understanding of how AI-generated voices and music differ from their human counterparts and the state-of-the-art techniques used to detect them.

In this chapter, we will cover the following topics:

- Navigating the world of AI-generated soundscapes.

- Detecting AI-generated auditory voices.

- From speech to melody: detecting AI-generated music.

- Watermarking as a solution for audio deepfake detection.

Technical requirements

To effectively follow along this chapter, particularly the example walkthroughs, ensure the following prerequisites are in place:

- Python 3.8 or later.

- Required Python libraries: `PyTorch` and `NumPy`.

Prepare your environment accordingly to gain hands-on experience with AI-generated audio and music detection techniques.

Navigating the world of AI-generated soundscapes

The rapid advancements in AI have revolutionized audio and music generation, creating profound implications for industries ranging from media and entertainment to cybersecurity. AI tools now produce synthetic voices indistinguishable from human speech and music compositions that rival human creativity in complexity and coherence. While these developments enable new opportunities for personalization, productivity, and creativity, they also bring significant risks, including audio deepfake scams, music plagiarism, and the erosion of trust in audio authenticity.

A stark illustration of the dangers posed by AI-generated deepfakes occurred when a finance worker at a multinational firm was deceived into transferring $25 million to fraudsters who impersonated the company's chief financial officer during a video conference call. The worker, believing he was interacting with genuine colleagues, was ultimately tricked into authorizing the substantial payout after the deepfake voices and appearances appeared convincing (Chen & Magramo, 2024). This incident show cases the sophisticated capabilities of AI in creating believable synthetic identities, highlighting the critical need for robust detection and verification methods to prevent such costly scams.

This chapter explores the evolving landscape of AI-generated audio and music, offering a comprehensive guide to discerning synthetic audio content. Targeted at industrial practitioners, it introduces cutting-edge detection techniques for AI-generated voice and music, and discusses watermarking as a powerful tool for verification and attribution. By the end, readers will gain actionable insights into combating misuse while leveraging AI technologies responsibly.

What's not covered?

This chapter focuses on AI-generated voices and music, addressing the technical, artistic, and ethical challenges associated with detecting and verifying synthetic speech and compositions. However, it does not cover the detection of *environmental sounds* (such as nature recordings, urban noise, or sound effects) generated or altered by AI systems, since they often lack the linguistic and musical structures that detection methods in this chapter rely on.

Additionally, this chapter does not tackle the *emotion-driven audio manipulations*, where AI alters existing audio to evoke specific emotions or create immersive experiences. These scenarios require distinct detection strategies that are beyond the scope of this discussion. Similarly, *speech-to-speech translation* and *language-specific audio synthesis* are excluded, as their detection mechanisms emphasize linguistic fidelity rather than audio authenticity.

By concentrating on AI-generated voices and music, this chapter seeks to deliver a focused and practical exploration of the current challenges and solutions in detection. This targeted approach aims to equip readers with insights into these specific areas while laying a foundation for understanding the broader landscape of AI-driven soundscapes.

Detecting AI-generated auditory voices

AI technologies, such as TTS and VC systems, have revolutionized voice synthesis, enabling the generation of human-like voices that are nearly indistinguishable from genuine recordings. For the purpose of this section, "auditory voices" refer specifically to human speech-like sounds generated by AI systems, including spoken words and vocal utterances, but excluding non-speech audio such as environmental noise, music, or other soundscapes. These advancements pose significant risks, including misuse in scams, misinformation, and identity fraud. Detecting AI-generated auditory voices has therefore become a critical challenge, requiring robust techniques to distinguish between human-produced and machine-generated speech. Voice deepfake detection involves two overarching strategies: **pipeline approaches** and **end-to-end systems**. Each offers unique capabilities and limitations.

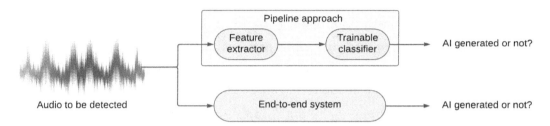

Figure 3.1. Main strategies for auditory voice detection: pipeline approaches and end-to-end systems.

Pipeline approaches combine an explicit feature extraction module, which processes raw audio to derive useful characteristics (features), with a **trainable** classifier that uses these features to determine whether the audio is real or fake (Yi et al., 2023; Li, Ahmadiadli, & Zhang, 2024). The extracted features can be largely categorized into *handcrafted* and *deep learning* features.

- Popular *handcrafted features* include many variants such as Mel-Frequency Cepstral Coefficients (MFCCs), Linear Frequency Cepstral Coefficients (LFCCs), and Constant-Q Transform spectrograms (CQTgram), to name a few. These features quantify patterns in audio, such as frequencies and their variations over time, helping to identify inconsistencies introduced by synthesis algorithms. For example, MFCCs simulate how human ears perceive sound frequencies (Chen, Guo & Dai, 2010), while LFCCs focus on linear frequency scales (Todisco et al., 2018), and CQTgram capture frequency information with high precision for lower tones (Cheng, Xu & Zheng, 2019). However, while effective for detecting certain anomalies, these features may struggle to generalize across diverse synthesis methods and environments (Zhang, Wen & Hu, 2024; Yang et al., 2024).

- *Deep Learning Features*: Recent works leverage multi-layer neural architectures such as SincNet (Ravanelli & Bengio, 2018) and Wav2Vec (Schneider et al., 2019; Baevski et al., 2020), which automatically learn discriminative features directly from audio. SincNet acts like a highly intelligent filter, designed to focus on specific sound details that matter most in distinguishing human voices from artificial ones, such as the unique qualities of a speaker's tone. Wav2Vec, on the other hand, listens to massive amounts of audio and learns to recognize subtle patterns and variations, like the pitch of a voice or how words are pronounced, making it particularly effective for tasks like audio deepfake detection (Yi et al., 2023).

End-to-end systems process raw audio directly, optimizing both feature extraction and classification in a single framework without relying on manually designed features. These systems can be categorized based on the core principles of their approach:

- *Convolution-based models*: These models use convolutional layers, which act like visual pattern detectors but are applied to sound, breaking the audio into small chunks and identifying key patterns or "fingerprints" in the waveforms. Muckenhirn et al. (2017) use a simple convolutional layer followed by dense (fully connected) layers to spot anomalies, while Dinkel et al. (2017) combines convolutional layers with LSTMs, which are specialized layers that act like memory units, helping the model "remember" how sounds evolve over time. ResNet-based architectures, such as Res-TSSDNet (Hua, Teoh & Zhang, 2021), take this further by using residual connections, which are shortcuts within the network that make deeper models easier to train, improving their accuracy across different datasets.

- *Raw waveform models* work directly on the raw audio signal without converting it into features like spectrograms. RawNet2 (Tak et al., 2021a) uses specialized filters, which are mathematical tools designed to focus on specific audio frequencies, to identify subtle differences between real and fake audio. An improved version, TO-RawNet (Wang et al., 2023), further enhances detection accuracy by refining how these filters capture unique patterns, ensuring better performance on challenging datasets.

- *Graph-Based Models* treat audio like a network of interconnected points, called a graph, where each point represents a specific feature of the sound. Jung et al. (2022) use graph attention mechanisms to focus on important connections within this network, helping it detect hard-to-spot inconsistencies in the audio. Tak et al. (2021b) build on this idea by combining multiple graphs that highlight different aspects of the sound, improving the system's ability to detect synthetic audio across varied conditions.

- *Transformer-Based Models*: Transformer is an advanced architecture that compares all parts of the audio to each other, looking for relationships across the entire recording. Rawformer (Liu et al., 2023) combines these transformers with convolutional layers to analyze both small, local patterns and broader, global inconsistencies in the audio. Liu et al. (2023) take this a step further by using squeeze-and-excitation layers, which help the model emphasize the most important feaaasitures while ignoring irrelevant noise, improving its ability to catch subtle artifacts in fake audio.

- *Differentiable Architecture Search Methods* automate the process of designing the network itself. Ge et al. (2021) uses a technique called differentiable architecture search, which tries out different network designs and parameters during training to find the best combination. This approach removes the need for human intervention, creating custom architectures that are highly optimized for detecting fake audio.

The end-to-end systems are trending in recent years due to their ability to jointly optimize feature extraction and classification. Here we use **AASIST** (Jung et al., 2022) as an example to walk through the training and testing process for an audio deepfake detection system on the ASVspoof dataset.

1. Clone the repository and navigate into the project directory

```
$ git clone https://github.com/clovaai/aasist.git
$ cd aasist
```

2. Install required dependencies.

```
$ pip install -r requirements.txt
```

3. Download the ASVspoof 2019 logical access dataset using the provided script or manually. Ensure the dataset is structured as expected.

```
$ python download_dataset.py
```

Alternatively, download and organize the dataset manually:

- Download LA.zip from https://datashare.ed.ac.uk/handle/10283/3336.
- Unzip the files and configure the dataset directory in the configuration file.

4. Inspect the configuration file that specifies model settings and dataset paths. For AASIST, open the default configuration file `AASIST.conf`.

```
$ vim config/AASIST.conf
```

Ensure the `dataset_path` points to the root of your ASVspoof dataset.

5. Run the training script with the specified configuration file. The script should automatically handle training, validation, and save model checkpoints.

```
$ python main.py --config ./config/AASIST.conf
```

6. To evaluate the model on the ASVspoof test set, use the `--eval` flag with the same configuration file.

```
$ python main.py --eval --config ./config/AASIST.conf
```

This outputs metrics such as EER (Equal Error Rate) and Min t-DCF (Minimum Tandem Detection Cost Function):

- EER shows how often the system gets confused when deciding whether an audio is real or fake. A lower EER means the system is better at making the right decision.
- Min t-DCF: measures how much the anti-spoofing system helps improve the overall reliability of a speaker verification system. Lower scores mean it works more effectively with speaker verification.

Challenges and emerging solutions

Despite progress, significant challenges persist. We will introduce several main challenges each with recent advancements that addresses the corresponding challenge.

Self-Supervised Learning (SSL) leverages pre-trained models trained on diverse datasets improves feature robustness. Models such as WavLM (Chen et al., 2022), HuBERT (Hsu et al., 2021), and Whisper (Radford et al., 2023) demonstrate exceptional generalization on unseen datasets by learning rich audio representations during pretraining.

Multi-feature incorporation methods, such as (Yang et al., 2024), combines features from different domains, such as spectral and temporal characteristics, enhances robustness. Feature fusion and selection mechanisms improve performance on varied synthesis techniques.

Ensemble models fuse multiple classifiers to enhance resilience against diverse deepfake generation technique (Pham et al., 2024).

Retrieval-augmented detection (RAD) frameworks (Kang et al., 2024) enhance detection by comparing input samples against similar examples in a knowledge base. This approach complements traditional classifiers by providing additional context.

Multi-dataset generalization: Current models often fail to perform well on unseen datasets or synthesis methods (Yi et al., 2023). Models trained on multi-dataset benchmarks, such as ASVspoof (Wang et al., 2020) and In-the-Wild (Müller et al., 2022), achieve better cross-domain performance by learning shared artifacts across synthesis methods.

Model calibration and reliability: Techniques to quantify uncertainty in predictions can improve trustworthiness in real-world deployments (Pascu et al., 2024b).

Adversarial robustness: Detection systems are vulnerable to perturbations, such as background noise or lossy compression, which can obscure synthetic artifacts (Yang et al., 2024; Pascu et al., 2024b).

Transparency and explainability: As detection models grow in complexity, ensuring their interpretability becomes critical for decision-making in sensitive contexts as demonstrated in (Zhang, Wen & Hu, 2024; Pascu et al., 2024a; Pascu et al., 2024b).

The detection of AI-generated voices remains a dynamic field. Innovations such as self-supervised learning, retrieval-augmented frameworks, and robust ensemble methods show promise in addressing existing gaps. However, achieving robustness against adversarial attacks and ensuring scalability across domains will require continued exploration and interdisciplinary collaboration. To stay informed about the latest research in this field, we recommend exploring the repository at https://github.com/john852517791/awesome-fake-audio-detection.

The use of free and commercial tooling

The aforementioned open-source methods and models are not user-friendly for most practical audiences; therefore, we provide examples of both free and commercial tools designed to identify AI-generated voices:

- **AI Voice Classifier** https://play.ht/voice-classifier-detect-ai-voices
  This tool analyzes audio files to determine if a voice is synthetic or human, assisting users in verifying the authenticity of voice recordings.

- **AI Speech Classifier** https://elevenlabs.io/ai-speech-classifier
  Specialized in detecting voices generated by ElevenLabs' text-to-speech technology, this classifier helps identify AI-produced speech.

- **AI Voice Detector** https://aivoicedetector.com
  Offering both a web interface and a browser extension, this tool enables users to upload audio files or analyze voices directly from platforms like YouTube, WhatsApp, TikTok, Zoom, and Google Meet. It detects AI-generated voices across various languages and accents, even in short audio clips.

- **Deepgram's AI Voice Detector** https://deepgram.com/ai-apps/ai-voice-detector
  Integrated into Deepgram's suite of AI applications, this detector assists in identifying AI-generated voices, ensuring the authenticity of audio content.

- **IDLive Voice Clone Detection** https://www.idrnd.ai/idlive-voice-clone-detection
  Designed to detect voice clones and audio deepfakes, this tool offers protection against identity fraud and misinformation by identifying AI-generated voices in audio samples.

- **Deepfake Voice Detector** https://en-gb.hiya.com/products/deepfake-voice-detector
  A free browser extension that utilizes advanced AI voice detection to verify if the voice in a video or audio clip is authentic or AI-generated, helping users spot misleading content and scams.

- **AI Speech Detector** https://www.ircamamplify.io/product/ai-voice-detector
  This tool ensures voice authenticity in audio clips, even if altered, by detecting AI-generated voices. It's particularly useful for journalists and media professionals to prevent engagement with deepfakes.

- **DeepFake-o-meter** https://zinc.cse.buffalo.edu/ubmdfl/deep-o-meter/landing_page
  An open platform integrating state-of-the-art deepfake detection methods, allowing users to upload audio samples to assess their authenticity.

To effectively use these AI voice detection tools, it is essential to adopt a systematic approach. One key strategy is cross-verification, meaning to test on multiple tools to analyze the same audio sample. Relying on a single tool may not provide comprehensive results, as different detectors might excel in identifying various aspects of synthetic voices. Additionally, attention to detail is crucial. Listen for unnatural speech patterns, such as consistent pitch, mechanical intonations, or the absence of natural pauses, which are common indicators of AI generation.

Regularly updating detection tools is another critical practice to ensure they remain effective against the latest AI technologies. Contextual analysis also plays a vital role; scrutinize the circumstances in which the audio is presented and flag unexpected or out-of-character statements for further evaluation. Finally, metadata examination can reveal anomalies or traces of synthetic generation, offering an additional layer of scrutiny. By combining these strategies, individuals and organizations can significantly improve their ability to detect and address the challenges posed by AI-generated voices.

From speech to melody: detecting AI-generated music

AI-Generated Music (AIGM) represents a significant technological advancement, enabling the automated creation of music compositions. Tools such as MuseNet (https://openai.com/research/musenet), Suno (https://suno.com), Mureka (https://www.mureka.ai), Soundful (https://soundful.com), Udio (https://udio.com), and AIVA (https://aiva.ai) have revolutionized the creative process by producing melodies, harmonies, and lyrics jointly at scale. However, the unregulated proliferation of AIGM raises concerns about originality, copyright infringement, and artistic authenticity. These challenges necessitate robust detection systems to differentiate between human-composed and machine-generated music (Li et al., 2024a; Li et al., 2024b).

Unlike voice or speech, music comprises a complex interplay of melody, harmony, rhythm, and lyrics, making the detection of AIGM especially challenging. Its subjective and interpretive nature, combined with a multimodal format that merges audio and lyrics, complicates standard detection methodologies. Consequently, current approaches to AIGM detection employ a range of analytical frameworks, machine learning techniques, and multimodal systems. These methods strive to pinpoint key distinctions between human-composed and machine-generated music across melody, harmony, rhythm, and lyrical dimensions. The core methods in AIGM detection include **feature-based analysis**, **end-to-end models**, and **multimodal approaches**.

Feature-based analysis relies on extracting specific characteristics of music for detection purposes. These features, often inspired by music theory, serve as the foundation for detecting irregularities in AI-generated compositions.

- *Melody* is the sequence of musical notes that forms the core identity of a piece of music. Human-created melodies typically display natural progressions and emotional depth, reflecting the composer's creativity and intent. In contrast, AI-generated melodies often lack variation or emotional resonance, sometimes appearing overly repetitive or rigid. Detection techniques analyze pitch, tone, and rhythmic flow to identify such synthetic patterns, distinguishing AI outputs from human compositions (Rao & Das, 2022).

- *Harmony* represents the combination of chords and chord progressions, adding depth and emotional nuance to music. AI-generated harmonies often differ from human-composed ones by being excessively structured or "mathematically perfect", which can feel unnatural. An example method for harmony detection is the Harmony-Aware Hierarchical Music Transformer (HAT), which leverages a structured approach to understand how chords transition in a piece of music. It builds a map of relationships between chords to catch patterns that might seem too mechanical or predictable, which are often signs of AI generation. Essentially, HAT helps identify when the harmony feels too precise to be human.

- *Rhythm* is the pattern of beats in music, giving it a sense of flow and timing. It's what makes you tap your foot or sway to a song. AI-generated rhythms sometimes feel too regular, like a drum machine, or may have sudden changes that break the natural flow. A method like **Perfect Authentic Cadence (PAC)** detection uses GNNs to find rhythm patterns that don't match human tendencies, such as overly predictable beats (Karystinaios & Widmer, 2022). Tools like **MrBERT (Li & Sung, 2023)** and **MusiConGen (Lan et al., 2024)**, which create music from text descriptions, include rhythm patterns as part of their process. By analyzing these patterns, we can spot irregularities that hint the rhythm might be machine-generated rather than naturally composed

- *Lyrics* often form a textual modality complementing music. Human-created lyrics tend to show contextual and emotional alignment with melodies, while AI-generated lyrics often lack depth or thematic congruence. Detection systems integrating pre-trained language models like BERT (Revathy et al., 2023) identify discrepancies between lyrics and music. Since lyrics are often generated by LLMs, readers are encouraged to refer to the methodologies introduced in Chapter 1 for more details.

End-to-end models offer an alternative approach by learning directly from raw audio data: the feature and classification is learned jointly. These systems are particularly suited for capturing intricate patterns and overarching structures in music, making them well-suited for detecting AI-generated music (AIGM).

- *CNNs* analyze spectrograms, extracting time-frequency domain features. Models like ResNet18 (Alzantot et al., 2019) and MobileNet (Wen et al., 2022) have demonstrated strong performance on datasets such as FakeMusicCaps (Comanducci, Bestagini, & Tubaro, 2024) by effectively identifying unique audio signatures. However, CNNs often struggle with generalization across out-of-domain datasets like M6 (Li et al., 2024c).

- *Transformer-based Models*: Transformers, known for their attention mechanisms, excel at modeling long-range dependencies, making them ideal for analyzing intricate musical compositions. Models like Vision Transformer (ViT) and Music Transformers (Huang et al., 2018) leverage attention mechanisms to model long-range dependencies in music. These models have shown promise but are computationally intensive and may require extensive fine-tuning for optimal performance (Li at al., 2024a).

- *Hybrid architectures*, which integrate different types of neural network layers, offer a powerful way to analyze music by leveraging the strengths of multiple approaches. Combining **CNNs** with recurrent layers like LSTM networks is particularly effective for capturing both spatial (texture) and temporal (flow) features. For example, the **CNN-LSTM model** proposed by Chen & Li (2020) identifies irregularities in extended compositions by analyzing complex melodic and harmonic progressions. However, hybrid architectures can go beyond CNNs. Models such as **Transformer-LSTM hybrids** use attention mechanisms alongside recurrent layers to capture long-range dependencies and temporal patterns in music, while **GNNs** combined with LSTMs can model relationships between musical components, such as chord transitions or thematic variations. These advanced configurations provide a more nuanced understanding of music's structure and dynamics, making them versatile tools for detecting AI-generated compositions in varied contexts.

Multimodal approaches: Music inherently combines multiple modalities, such as audio (melody, harmony, rhythm) and text (lyrics), making its analysis particularly complex. Multimodal approaches aim to leverage information from these diverse sources to enhance detection accuracy by capturing the interplay between modalities. These methods are broadly categorized into four types based on *when and how* the features are combined within the detection model: *early fusion, late fusion, intermediate fusion*, and *hierarchical fusion*.

- *Early fusion techniques*: Early fusion integrates features from multiple modalities (e.g., melody and lyrics) at the input stage. These features are concatenated and fed into a unified model for joint processing. For example, Wav2Vec2.0 (Baevski et al., 2020) extracts audio features, while BERT processes lyrics; their outputs are combined for classification. Li et al. (2024b) demonstrated that this approach significantly outperformed unimodal systems, achieving an accuracy of 0.975 on subsets of the M6 dataset.

- *Late fusion* processes each modality independently, with separate models analyzing features like melody and lyrics. Their predictions are then combined using methods like weighted averaging or majority voting. For example, **Li et al. (2024c)** used separate classifiers for audio and text, merging outputs through weighted voting, ensuring that each modality receives specialized attention while maintaining simplicity in the fusion process. This method is advantageous for modular designs but may fail to capture deeper cross-modal relationships

- *Intermediate fusion* combines features at different stages of processing, allowing the model to capture interactions between modalities during computation. An example is the **Multimodal Transformer (MMT)** by Tsai et al. (2019), which uses attention mechanisms to integrate features extracted by CNNs (for melody) and Transformers (for lyrics). This approach provides a richer representation by balancing the simplicity of early fusion with the modularity of late fusion.

- *Hierarchical fusion architecture* represents a kind of advanced systems that are specifically designed to handle the structured nature of music, such as verses and choruses. They model temporal and contextual dependencies between different sections, aligning musical elements with lyrics at multiple levels. For instance, **Hierarchical Multimodal Music Model (HMMM)** by Wang et al. (2024) captures relationships between lyrics and musical elements by employing hierarchical attention layers, enabling improved interpretability and cross-modal analysis.

Challenges and trends in AIGM detection

The detection of AIGM presents unique challenges that blend technical, artistic, and computational aspects. These challenges highlight the gaps in current methodologies and datasets, offering directions for future advancements. Below, we outline the primary challenges and emerging trends in this field.

A key challenge in AIGM detection is the **limited generalization capability** of models across different datasets. Models trained on specific datasets, such as **FakeMusicCaps**, often perform poorly when tested on out-of-domain data like the **M6 dataset**. For instance, while MobileNet demonstrated strong results on FakeMusicCaps, its accuracy significantly dropped in out-of-domain scenarios, emphasizing the need for robust generalization strategies. Future solutions may involve domain adaptation techniques, which enable models to learn invariant features transferable across datasets, or ensemble methods that combine insights from multiple training sets.

The **diversity of datasets** plays a crucial role in the robustness of AIGM detection models. Existing datasets often fail to capture the broad spectrum of musical styles, cultural contexts, and instrumentation. **FakeMusicCaps** provides a rich collection of over 27,000 machine-generated tracks and 5,000 human-composed pieces, but its focus on background music limits its scope. The **SONICS dataset** (Rahman et al., 2024), with its integration of lyrics and melodies, offers a multimodal perspective but still falls short in representing global cultural and genre variations. Expanding datasets to include more diverse genres, instruments, and cultural influences is essential for building more comprehensive detection systems.

Integrating audio and text features, a necessity in multimodal AIGM detection, introduces additional **multimodal complexity**. Lyrics often diverge from standard language patterns, requiring specialized NLP models. Misalignment between textual and auditory modalities can hinder the performance of detection systems. Advanced fusion techniques, such as the intermediate and hierarchical fusion introduced previously, offer promising solutions by capturing nuanced interactions between lyrics and music. However, these approaches demand high computational resources and careful design to ensure accurate alignment.

Explainability is becoming increasingly critical in AIGM detection, as stakeholders demand transparency in model decisions. Integrated Gradients (Sundararajan et al., 2017), which measures changes in model output along a path from baseline to input, helps identify critical regions in music that influence classification outcomes. Similarly, Grad-CAM (Selvaraju et al., 2017) visualizes gradients across spectrograms to highlight time-frequency regions most relevant to a model's decisions. The colored areas in Figure 3.2 show case those critical regions that has high impact on discerning the input music spectrograms. These methods not only build trust in detection systems but also guide the development of more interpretable models.

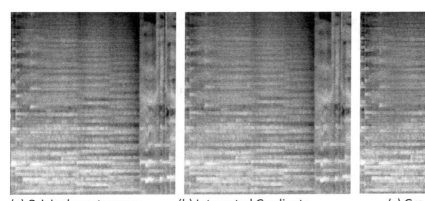

(a) Original spectrogram　　(b) Integrated Gradients　　(c) Grad-CAM

Figure 3.2. Visualization of critical regions in music spectrogram that influence the classification outcomes.

Detection systems face threats from **adversarial attacks** that subtly modify music to deceive classifiers. For instance, noise addition or tempo alteration can obscure key features that models rely on for accurate classification. Existing models like ResNet and MobileNet exhibit vulnerabilities to such manipulations. Incorporating adversarial training and resilience-focused architectures could enhance robustness, making systems more reliable under real-world conditions.

In conclusion, while this section does not provide a detailed walkthrough of a specific AI-generated music detection example, it's noteworthy that many techniques overlap with those used in audio deepfake detection, particularly when employing spectrogram inputs. The AASIST model, previously discussed, can be adapted for music detection tasks. However, publicly available tools for detecting AI-generated music are currently limited. Innovative approaches, such as altering a track's speed using tools like TimeStretch (https://29a.ch/timestretch), may help identify AI-generated characteristics. Additionally, platforms like AI Music Detector (https://www.ircamamplify.io/product/ai-generated-music-detector) offer specialized services to detect AI-generated tracks at scale, aiming to maintain a fair and transparent environment for music consumption on streaming platforms.

Watermarking as a solution for audio deepfake detection

Watermarking is an emerging solution in the detection and identification of AI-generated audio, offering a robust mechanism to differentiate synthetic from authentic content. While widely used in digital copyright protection, its application in detecting audio deepfakes and AI-generated music presents unique challenges and opportunities. By embedding imperceptible markers within audio signals, watermarking provides a method for ensuring authenticity, verifying authorship, and enhancing trust in digital audio ecosystems. However, its implementation varies significantly between music detection and voice detection due to the distinct nature and requirements of these domains.

Role and purpose of watermarking

Watermarking in music detection primarily serves the purpose of authorship verification and copyright protection. It ensures that a musical composition can be accurately attributed to its rightful creator, whether human or AI-generated. This is particularly critical in creative industries, where protecting intellectual property rights is essential to prevent unauthorized reuse, misattribution, or plagiarism. By embedding imperceptible markers in music, watermarking safeguards the integrity and originality of artistic work.

In voice detection, watermarking plays a vital role in identifying synthetic speech and distinguishing it from human-generated audio. This capability is crucial for ensuring the trustworthiness of voice-based communications, particularly in authentication systems and speaker verification. Applications extend to security systems and forensic investigations, where maintaining audio integrity is paramount to preventing fraud or misuse. By embedding unique identifiers, watermarking enhances the reliability of voice data in high-stakes environment.

Nature of the embedded watermarks

Watermarks in music are embedded within core musical attributes such as rhythm, harmony, or timbre, ensuring they remain imperceptible to listeners while preserving artistic integrity. These watermarks must be resilient to creative transformations like remixes, tempo changes, and genre shifts, which are common in music production and re-arrangements. For example, subtle rhythmic changes or modifications to chord transitions in symbolic music scores (e.g., MIDI files) serve as effective yet unobtrusive methods for embedding watermarks, blending seamlessly with the musical composition.

In voice detection, watermarks are typically embedded as subtle spectral distortions, phase shifts, or inaudible high-frequency tones. They are designed to survive transmission distortions, such as noise, compression, or telecommunication artifacts, without compromising the naturalness of speech. For instance, unique metadata or phoneme duration modulations can be introduced as identifiers, ensuring that the watermark remains detectable even after significant processing or environmental interference.

Methods of embedding watermarks

In music, watermarking can be applied at two primary levels: symbolic and audio. *Symbolic watermarks* are embedded directly into the musical score, such as slight alterations to note durations, rhythmic patterns, or harmonic progressions. These changes are subtle enough to go unnoticed by listeners while still carrying identifying information. For example, in MIDI files, harmonic transitions can be slightly modified to embed a unique marker without disrupting the overall flow and feel of the music. On the *audio level*, watermarks are applied during production or mastering stages, where imperceptible phase or amplitude changes are introduced into the waveform. These modifications blend seamlessly with the natural audio characteristics of the music, ensuring the watermark remains intact while resisting degradation from typical transformations like remixes, tempo shifts, or genre adaptations.

Watermarking in voice detection typically involves spectral and temporal modifications to the audio signal. *Spectral watermarks* introduce subtle changes to the frequency domain, such as minor phase shifts or inaudible modulations in high-frequency ranges. These modifications are designed to embed unique identifiers into the voice while being imperceptible to human ears. *Temporal watermarks*, on the other hand, focus on altering the timing of speech elements, such as adjusting phoneme durations or introducing minute variations in pauses. These alterations are carefully crafted to avoid disrupting the natural flow and intelligibility of speech. The primary goal of these methods is to ensure the watermarks can survive environmental distortions, compression, and noise while remaining detectable by algorithmic analysis.

Detection and extraction mechanisms

Watermark extraction and verification in music require robust machine learning models that align embedded markers with key musical features such as melody, harmony, or rhythm. These systems must also handle transformations commonly applied in music, including tempo changes, remixes, or pitch shifts, which can obscure or distort the embedded watermarks.

In voice-based detection, signal processing and spectral analysis are used to extract watermarks from audio, even in challenging environments with compression or noise. Real-time detection capabilities are often essential for applications such as speaker authentication or live broadcasts, ensuring the integrity and authenticity of audio in dynamic settings.

Here is a simple walkthrough demonstrating how to embed a watermark into an audio file with **AudioSeal** (San Roman et al., 2024) and then detect it. We use a single example audio file called `speech_example.wav`. This tutorial focuses on inference only (embedding and detection). It is possible to train or fine-tune your own models, but we won't cover that here.

1. Install AudioSeal.

```
$ pip install audioseal
```

2. Import libraries and load an example audio file `speech_example.wav`. If you do not have an audio file by your hand, you can choose to download any audio clip from https://pierrefdz.github.io/publications/audioseal.

```python
import torch
import torchaudio
from audioseal import AudioSeal

audio_file = "speech_example.wav"
wav, sr = torchaudio.load(audio_file)
```

3. Load the watermark generator model.

```python
generator = AudioSeal.load_generator("audioseal_wm_16bits")
```

4. Generate an imperceptible watermark.

```python
watermark = generator.get_watermark(wav, sr)
```

5. Add the generated watermark to the original audio.

```python
watermarked_audio = wav + watermark
```

6. Load the watermark detection model.

```python
detector =
AudioSeal.load_detector("audioseal_detector_16bits")
```

7. Run detection on the previously watermarked audio.

```
result, message =
detector.detect_watermark(watermarked_audio, sr)
```

8. Print and interpret the watermark detection result.

```
print(f"Probability of watermark presence: {result:.4f}")

print(f"Detected 16-bit message: {message}")
```

`result` is a float value between 0 and 1 indicating the probability that the audio is watermarked. `message` is the extracted 16-bit (optional) identifier if watermark is present.

9. (Optional) Save watermarked audio.

```
torchaudio.save("speech_example_watermarked.wav",
  watermarked_audio, sample_rate=sr)
```

That's it! You've successfully embedded a watermark into `speech_example.wav` and then detected it. If you wish to customize or train your own generator/detector, please refer to the official document (https://github.com/facebookresearch/audioseal) for more details.

Robustness and limitations

Watermarks in music must withstand a variety of artistic transformations, such as transpositions, remixes, and changes in genre. These modifications can alter the original structure and elements of a piece, posing challenges for the detection and extraction of embedded watermarks. Additionally, there is a risk of subjectivity, where musical variations introduced by creative processes might unintentionally mask or distort the watermark, complicating verification efforts.

Watermarks in voice-based detection face distinct technical challenges, including degradation caused by speech compression formats like MP3 and AAC, as well as environmental noise. Furthermore, advanced AI techniques, such as diffusion models for generating synthetic speech, can inadvertently erase or obscure the embedded watermarks during the synthesis process. These challenges underscore the need for robust watermarking methods that maintain their integrity across a range of real-world condition.

Ethical and legal considerations

In the context of music detection, embedding watermarks must carefully balance artistic integrity to avoid distorting the creative intent of composers. These watermarks can serve as a vital legal tool in copyright disputes, helping artists establish authorship and combat plagiarism. However, any unintended alteration to the musical quality could raise concerns among creators about the authenticity of their works.

For voice detection, watermarking raises significant privacy and surveillance concerns, as it may be used to track users or identify speakers without their consent. In forensic or authentication systems, the misuse of watermarked audio could lead to ethical challenges, particularly in sensitive or high-stakes scenarios where the accuracy and intention of detection mechanisms are critical.

Comparative summary

Watermarking serves as a versatile tool in detecting AI-generated audio and music, but its implementation differs significantly between music detection and voice detection due to their distinct characteristics and objectives. While music watermarking emphasizes creative integrity and resilience against artistic transformations, voice watermarking focuses on robustness against technical distortions and real-world noise. The table below outlines these key distinctions:

Aspect	Music detection	Auditory voice detection
Purpose	Authorship verification, copyright protection	Differentiating synthetic vs. real speech
Watermark type	Rhythm, harmony, timbre, frequency	Spectral distortions, timing shifts, metadata
Embedding label	Symbolic (score) or audio (waveform)	Temporal and spectral domains
Challenges	Artistic integrity, genre diversity	Robustness to compression and noise
Detection tools	Machine learning with musicological alignment	Signal processing, ML for spectral analysis

By tailoring watermarking methods to the specific needs of music and voice detection, these frameworks can achieve greater resilience and effectiveness in safeguarding the authenticity and integrity of digital audio content.

Summary

This chapter explored the multifaceted domain of AI-generated audio and music, emphasizing the profound technological advancements that enable synthetic speech and music creation. It addressed the dual-edged impact of these technologies, highlighting the innovative possibilities alongside the significant risks, such as deepfake scams and music plagiarism. Through sections on detecting AI-generated voices and music, the chapter presented cutting-edge techniques, from feature-based and multimodal approaches to end-to-end models, and underscored the challenges of domain generalization and dataset diversity. Additionally, watermarking was introduced as a robust solution for verifying authenticity and protecting intellectual property across music and voice applications. By equipping readers with actionable insights, practical examples and technical tools, this chapter aims to empower readers to responsibly navigate and mitigate the challenges posed by AI-driven soundscapes.

References

Chen, H., & Magramo, K. (2024, February 4). *Finance worker pays out $25 million after video call with deepfake 'chief financial officer'*. CNN. https://edition.cnn.com/2024/02/04/asia/deepfake-cfo-scam-hong-kong-intl-hnk.

Yi, J., Wang, C., Tao, J., Zhang, X., Zhang, C. Y., & Zhao, Y. (2023). Audio deepfake detection: A survey. arXiv preprint arXiv:2308.14970.

Li, M., Ahmadiadli, Y., & Zhang, X.-P. (2024). Audio anti-spoofing detection: A survey. *arXiv preprint arXiv:2404.13914*.

Li, S., & Sung, Y. (2023). MrBERT: Pre-training of melody and rhythm for automatic music generation. *Mathematics, 11*(4), 798. MDPI.

Lan, Y.-H., Hsiao, W.-Y., Cheng, H.-C., & Yang, Y.-H. (2024). Musicogen: Rhythm and chord control for transformer-based text-to-music generation. *arXiv preprint arXiv:2407.15060*.

Zhang, Q., Wen, S., & Hu, T. (2024). Audio deepfake detection with self-supervised XLS-R and SLS classifier. In *Proceedings of the 32nd ACM International Conference on Multimedia* (pp. 6765–6773).

Zhang, X., Zhang, J., Qiu, Y., Wang, L., & Zhou, J. (2022). Structure-enhanced pop music generation via harmony-aware learning. In *Proceedings of the 30th ACM International Conference on Multimedia* (pp. 1204–1213).

Yang, Y., Qin, H., Zhou, H., Wang, C., Guo, T., Han, K., & Wang, Y. (2024). A robust audio deepfake detection system via multi-view feature. In *ICASSP 2024-2024 IEEE International Conference on Acoustics, Speech and Signal Processing (ICASSP)* (pp. 13131–13135). IEEE.

Schneider, S., Baevski, A., Collobert, R., & Auli, M. (2019). Wav2vec: Unsupervised pre-training for speech recognition. *Interspeech 2019*. ISCA.

Sundararajan, M., Taly, A., & Yan, Q. (2017). Axiomatic attribution for deep networks. In *International Conference on Machine Learning* (pp. 3319–3328). PMLR.

Selvaraju, R. R., Cogswell, M., Das, A., Vedantam, R., Parikh, D., & Batra, D. (2017). Grad-CAM: Visual explanations from deep networks via gradient-based localization. In *Proceedings of the IEEE International Conference on Computer Vision* (pp. 618–626).

Baevski, A., Zhou, Y., Mohamed, A., & Auli, M. (2020). wav2vec 2.0: A framework for self-supervised learning of speech representations. *Advances in Neural Information Processing Systems*, 33, 12449–12460.

Ravanelli, M., & Bengio, Y. (2018). Speaker recognition from raw waveform with SincNet. In *2018 IEEE Spoken Language Technology Workshop (SLT)* (pp. 1021–1028). IEEE.

Pascu, O., Stan, A., Oneata, D., Oneata, E., & Cucu, H. (2024a). Towards generalisable and calibrated audio deepfake detection with self-supervised representations. In *Proceedings of Interspeech 2024* (pp. 4828–4832).

Chen, S., Wang, C., Chen, Z., Wu, Y., Liu, S., Chen, Z., Li, J., Kanda, N., Yoshioka, T., Xiao, X., & others. (2022). WavLM: Large-scale self-supervised pre-training for full-stack speech processing. *IEEE Journal of Selected Topics in Signal Processing*, 16(6), 1505–1518. IEEE.

Chen, C., & Li, Q. (2020). A multimodal music emotion classification method based on a multifeature combined network classifier. *Mathematical Problems in Engineering*, 2020(1), 4606027. Wiley Online Library.

Hsu, W.-N., Bolte, B., Tsai, Y.-H. H., Lakhotia, K., Salakhutdinov, R., & Mohamed, A. (2021). Hubert: Self-supervised speech representation learning by masked prediction of hidden units. *IEEE/ACM Transactions on Audio, Speech, and Language Processing*, 29, 3451–3460. IEEE.

Radford, A., Kim, J. W., Xu, T., Brockman, G., McLeavey, C., & Sutskever, I. (2023). Robust speech recognition via large-scale weak supervision. In *International Conference on Machine Learning* (pp. 28492–28518). PMLR.

Pham, L., Lam, P., Nguyen, T., Nguyen, H., & Schindler, A. (2024). Deepfake audio detection using spectrogram-based features and ensemble of deep learning models. In *2024 IEEE 5th International Symposium on the Internet of Sounds (IS2)* (pp. 1–5). IEEE.

Kang, Z., He, Y., Zhao, B., Qu, X., Peng, J., Xiao, J., & Wang, J. (2024). Retrieval-augmented audio deepfake detection. In *Proceedings of the 2024 International Conference on Multimedia Retrieval* (pp. 376–384).

Karystinaios, E., & Widmer, G. (2022). Cadence detection in symbolic classical music using graph neural networks. In *ISMIR 2022 Hybrid Conference*.

Wang, X., Yamagishi, J., Todisco, M., Delgado, H., Nautsch, A., Evans, N., Sahidullah, M., Vestman, V., Kinnunen, T., Lee, K. A., & others. (2020). ASVspoof 2019: A large-scale public database of synthesized, converted and replayed speech. *Computer Speech & Language, 64*, 101114. Elsevier.

Müller, N., Czempin, P., Diekmann, F., Froghyar, A., & Böttinger, K. (2022). Does audio deepfake detection generalize? *Interspeech 2022*. ISCA.

Pascu, O., Oneata, D., Cucu, H., & Müller, N. M. (2024b). Easy, interpretable, effective: openSMILE for voice deepfake detection. *arXiv preprint arXiv:2408.15775*.

Li, Y., Milling, M., Specia, L., & Schuller, B. W. (2024a). to AI-generated music detection: A pathway and overview. *arXiv preprint arXiv:2412.00571*.

Li, Y., Sun, Q., Li, H., Specia, L., & Schuller, B. W. (2024b). Detecting machine-generated music with explainability: A challenge and early benchmarks. *arXiv preprint arXiv:2412.13421*.

Li, Y., Li, H., Specia, L., & Schuller, B. W. (2024c). M6: Multi-generator, multi-domain, multi-lingual and cultural, multi-genres, multi-instrument machine-generated music detection databases. *arXiv preprint arXiv:2412.06001*.

Huang, C.-Z. A., Vaswani, A., Uszkoreit, J., Simon, I., Hawthorne, C., Shazeer, N., Dai, A. M., Hoffman, M. D., Dinculescu, M., & Eck, D. (2018). Music Transformer: Generating music with long-term structure. In *International Conference on Learning Representations*.

Rao, K. S., & Das, P. P. (2022). Melody extraction from polyphonic music by deep learning approaches: A review. *arXiv preprint arXiv:2202.01078*.

Revathy, V. R., Pillai, A. S., & Daneshfar, F. (2023). LyEmoBERT: Classification of lyrics' emotion and recommendation using a pre-trained model. *Procedia Computer Science, 218*, 1196–1208. Elsevier.

Rahman, M. A., Hakim, Z. I. A., Sarker, N. H., Paul, B., & Fattah, S. A. (2024). SONICS: Synthetic or not—Identifying counterfeit songs. *arXiv preprint arXiv:2408.14080*.

Wen, Y., Lei, Z., Yang, Y., Liu, C., & Ma, M. (2022). Multi-path GMM-MobileNet based on attack algorithms and codecs for synthetic speech and deepfake detection. In *Proceedings of Interspeech 2022* (pp. 4795–4799).

Alzantot, M., Wang, Z., & Srivastava, M. B. (2019). Deep residual neural networks for audio spoofing detection. *arXiv preprint arXiv:1907.00501*.

Comanducci, L., Bestagini, P., & Tubaro, S. (2024). Fakemusiccaps: A dataset for detection and attribution of synthetic music generated via text-to-music models. *arXiv preprint arXiv:2409.10684*.

Chen, L.-W., Guo, W., & Dai, L.-R. (2010). Speaker verification against synthetic speech. In *2010 7th International Symposium on Chinese Spoken Language Processing* (pp. 309–312). IEEE.

Cheng, X., Xu, M., & Zheng, T. F. (2019). Replay detection using CQT-based modified group delay feature and ResNeWt network in ASVspoof 2019. In *2019 Asia-Pacific Signal and Information Processing Association Annual Summit and Conference (APSIPA ASC)* (pp. 540–545). IEEE.

Todisco, M., Delgado, H., Lee, K. A., Sahidullah, M., Evans, N., Kinnunen, T., & Yamagishi, J. (2018). Integrated presentation attack detection and automatic speaker verification: Common features and Gaussian back-end fusion. In *Interspeech 2018–19th Annual Conference of the International Speech Communication Association*. ISCA.

Dinkel, H., Chen, N., Qian, Y., & Yu, K. (2017). End-to-end spoofing detection with raw waveform CLDNNs. In *2017 IEEE International Conference on Acoustics, Speech and Signal Processing (ICASSP)* (pp. 4860–4864). IEEE.

Hua, G., Teoh, A. B. J., & Zhang, H. (2021). Towards end-to-end synthetic speech detection. *IEEE Signal Processing Letters, 28*, 1265–1269. IEEE.

Tak, H., Patino, J., Todisco, M., Nautsch, A., Evans, N., & Larcher, A. (2021a). End-to-end anti-spoofing with RawNet2. In *ICASSP 2021-2021 IEEE International Conference on Acoustics, Speech and Signal Processing (ICASSP)* (pp. 6369–6373). IEEE.

Tak, H., Jung, J., Patino, J., Kamble, M., Todisco, M., & Evans, N. (2021b). End-to-end spectro-temporal graph attention networks for speaker verification anti-spoofing and speech deepfake detection. *arXiv preprint arXiv:2107.12710*.

Tsai, Y.-H. H., Bai, S., Liang, P. P., Kolter, J. Z., Morency, L.-P., & Salakhutdinov, R. (2019). Multimodal transformer for unaligned multimodal language sequences. In *Proceedings of the Conference. Association for Computational Linguistics. Meeting* (Vol. 2019, p. 6558). NIH Public Access.

Wang, C., Yi, J., Tao, J., Zhang, C., Zhang, S., Fu, R., & Chen, X. (2023). TO-Rawnet: Improving RawNet with TCN and orthogonal regularization for fake audio detection. *arXiv preprint arXiv:2305.13701*.

Wang, J., Sharifi, A., Gadekallu, T. R., & Shankar, A. (2024). MMD-MII model: A multilayered analysis and multimodal integration interaction approach revolutionizing music emotion classification. *International Journal of Computational Intelligence Systems, 17*(1), 99. Springer.

Jung, J., Heo, H.-S., Tak, H., Shim, H.-J., Chung, J. S., Lee, B.-J., Yu, H.-J., & Evans, N. (2022). AASIST: Audio anti-spoofing using integrated spectro-temporal graph attention networks. In *ICASSP 2022-2022 IEEE International Conference on Acoustics, Speech and Signal Processing (ICASSP)* (pp. 6367–6371). IEEE.

Liu, X., Liu, M., Wang, L., Lee, K. A., Zhang, H., & Dang, J. (2023). Leveraging positional-related local-global dependency for synthetic speech detection. In *ICASSP 2023-2023 IEEE International Conference on Acoustics, Speech and Signal Processing (ICASSP)* (pp. 1–5). IEEE.

Ge, W., Patino, J., Todisco, M., & Evans, N. (2021). Raw differentiable architecture search for speech deepfake and spoofing detection. In *ASVSPOOF 2021: Automatic Speaker Verification and Spoofing Countermeasures Challenge* (pp. 22–28). ISCA.

Muckenhirn, H., Magimai-Doss, M., & Marcel, S. (2017). End-to-end convolutional neural network-based voice presentation attack detection. In *2017 IEEE International Joint Conference on Biometrics (IJCB)* (pp. 335–341). IEEE.

San Roman, R., Fernandez, P., Elsahar, H., Défosséz, A., Furon, T., & Tran, T. (2024). Proactive detection of voice cloning with localized watermarking. In *International Conference on Machine Learning* (Vol. 235).

www.ingramcontent.com/pod-product-compliance
Lightning Source LLC
LaVergne TN
LVHW062035060326
832903LV00062B/1725